U.N.I.Q.U.E.
GROWING THE LEADER WITHIN

By Debra J. Slover

LEADER
GARDEN
PRESS

LEADERSHIP GARDEN™ LEGACY

Every person is a unique seed

in the world's garden.

Each seed grows a leader

from which greatness can blossom.

Imagine the future of our planet

if we nurture each leader

to sprout greatness.

— Debra J. Slover

Book cover and interior design by *1106 Design*
Illustration by *Darlene Warner*
Editing by *Writers Welcome*
Photo by *Alisha Hay*

The author of this book does not dispense medical advice or prescribe the use of any
technique as a form of physical, emotional, or medical problems without the advice
of a physician, either directly or indirectly. The intent of the author is only to offer
information of an educational and general nature. In the event you use any of the
information in this book for yourself, which is your constitutional right, the author
and the publisher assume no responsibility for your actions.

Library of Congress Control Number: 2006909896

Soft Cover:
ISBN-13: 978-097867980-4
ISBN-10: 0-97867980-6

Hard Cover:
ISBN-13: 978-097867981-1
ISBN-10: 097867981-4

First Edition

Manufactured in the U.S.A.

Special editions, including personalized covers, excerpts, and corporate imprints,
can be created in large quantities for special needs. For information about special
discounts for bulk purchases, sales promotions, or premiums please contact special
sales at Leader Garden Press: order@leadergardenpress.com

CONTENTS

Prologue   vii
Introduction   xi

Part One – Welcome to the Leadership Farm   1
1 – Leadership Garden   3
2 – Planting a Leadership Garden   15

Part Two – The U.N.I.Q.U.E. Tour Begins   29
3 – Understanding Field   35
4 – Nurturing Meadow   55
5 – Inventive Roost   73
6 – Quality Yard   91
7 – Unstoppable Pasture   105
8 – Expression Pen   119

Epilogue   137
Acknowledgements   141
Appendices:
    The Future—Empower the Seeds of
        Leadership Greatness   143
    About the Author   147

PROLOGUE

The conference is in its second day. Actress and author Mariette Hartley is at the podium, sharing her battle with alcohol, bipolar disorder, and her father's suicide when she was only twenty-three. Though I thought by now I was immune to the sad and tragic stories told at these conferences, I realize hers is all too familiar. Mariette says something about children who grow up in families like this often spend their lives trying to make sense out of that which makes no sense. The floodgates to my soul open and I begin to cry.

After her speech, I go up and speak to her, barely able to get the words out. "We were the same age when one of our parents died by suicide," I tell her.

She puts her arms around me. "I'll bet you've never heard your story told before," she says. I nod my head.

My attempt to make sense of my mother's suicide ends that day. I begin to heal in unknown places and a new freedom to express my love, passion, and commitment in life begins to surface after 25 years.

As a child, I never knew what to expect when I came home from school. Would my mother have dinner on the table, be out playing cards with her friends, in bed with another bout of depression, or watching TV in her bathrobe, her mind off in some distant place? On her good days, my mother was a brilliant, creative, and vivacious woman. Her personality could light up any room. She never knew a stranger and everyone loved her. I knew she loved me but I also knew there was something deep inside her that I never understood.

Dad seemed like the stable one, unless he'd had a few drinks. Then the chaos would begin. Family holidays and outings were ruined. Our parents would always apologize and promise to make it up to my brother and me—but they never could. The chaos in our family became our little secret.

As I approached adolescence, I realized Mom was beginning to live her life through me. I found that pleasing her was a way to keep her depression at bay, pulling us both into an unhealthy circle of deception.

One day, after I'd graduated from college, I got a call from my older brother. "She's probably not going to make it this time," he told me. This was not our mother's first suicide attempt, but it would be her last.

Before she died, I sat by her bedside and asked her, "Why?"

"To set your father free," she said quietly. She didn't explain, I didn't ask, and then she was gone. That day, I vowed to never lose sight of myself.

Although I wanted a life unlike my mother's, I found myself repeating my family patterns: an unhappy marriage, arguments, drinking, and family secrets—a mirror to my childhood, except I had a career I loved, teaching youth leadership skills to promote safe and healthy behaviors. My job became the subsistence of my life, but my private life remained my secret. I was a busy woman and, unlike my mother, I refused to lie in bed, depressed about my unhappiness at home.

After 20 years of living that secret life, I divorced my husband. I chose to start over and take personal responsibility for my happiness, rather than have it be dependent upon circumstances or other people. I eventually remarried and created the life I had always wanted with my children and new husband. I had accomplished what my mother never could.

I should have been joyous, but the funding for my youth program was in jeopardy and every day I feared the elimination of the program and my job. I realized my identity had been wrapped up in my career, just like my mother's identity had been wrapped up in me.

I refused to let the demise of my job ruin my new life, or my career. I continued in leadership development and started my own company. The work was the same, but my leadership style had shifted from surviving to thriving. I had become a happy and fulfilled woman with my career and home life now aligned. Finally, there were no more secrets and no need to hide.

I've learned that creating a purpose in life ignites our spirit and imagination and lets us experience life as a fully expressed leader. Being responsible for that spirit gives us the freedom to thrive, creating our own unique legacy of leadership.

I've often wondered what life would've been like for my mother if she had discovered her leader spirit within, but I'll never know. I wrote this book in her memory, as a voice to empower extraordinary unstoppable leadership in life.

— *Debra J. Slover*

INTRODUCTION

True leadership is not a title, position, or job. It's a way of life that expresses our imagination, purpose, and spirit. What brings those qualities to life is unique in everyone. *U.N.I.Q.U.E: Growing the Leader Within*, gives you a new view of leadership, using a garden metaphor to help you *tap* into your imagination, dreams, and spirit. All plants have a primary shoot called the leader, which eventually blooms. Like plants, each person is a leader waiting to blossom.

I developed the acronym, U.N.I.Q.U.E. as the Understanding, Nurturing, Inventive, Quality, Unstoppable, Expression of leadership to help grow the leader within. In this book, you'll learn how to connect the heart, mind, and spirit in a new way by planting a Leadership Garden™. I created the Leadership Farm fable as a teaching tool to convey the principles and practices of Leadership Gardens.

The fable begins when Hugh, a lost sheep who represents the heart, mind, and spirit in each of us, wanders onto the Leadership Farm. Each character he meets represents an aspect of the journey: Leda, a nurturing and compassionate gardener; her husband Aristotle, our purpose and aim; and Annabelle, a Border collie, the favor, grace, and beauty of life.

Annabelle takes Hugh to meet the other animals on the farm to learn the Leadership Garden principles. With Hugh, you'll plant new seeds, uproot weeds, and learn leader-friendly gardening practices that allow your unique leader to thrive.

Each chapter opens with Hugh and one or more of the characters, transitions to a lesson using my own experiences, then returns to Hugh and the characters for review. Reader exercises are at the end of each chapter. My hope is that this book will provide value, entertain, and enliven you. Whether you are a parent, teacher, counselor, coach, grandparent, faith leader, civic leader, employee, or employer, unearthing your unique leader spirit will increase your capacity to have a positive impact upon those around you.

I've learned that it is not life's circumstances that destroys goals and dreams, but our dampened spirit. I've used my own life to illustrate that even through tragedy and hardship, our leader spirit can emerge.

In the end, true leadership is not measured by what we do, or what we achieve, but by who we are. And it's understanding the value of who we are that makes a positive difference in our lives and the lives of those around us.

So let's get started.

PART ONE

WELCOME TO THE LEADERSHIP FARM

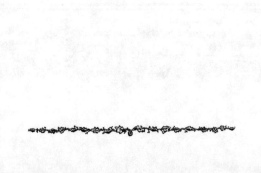

LEADERSHIP
GARDEN

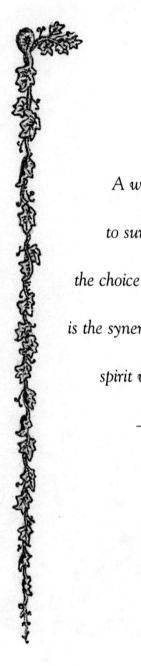

A weed takes little effort

to survive in a garden, yet

the choice to grow a thriving garden

is the synergy of the heart, mind, and

spirit with purpose and aim.

— Debra J. Slover

It's an early spring morning; the sun is rising in the east. Leda is on the front porch of her farmhouse drinking tea—a cool breeze blows through her hair. She thinks of her new garden. *I love this season. It is my time of hope, anticipation, and renewal.*

Leda sets aside her tea and heads to the garden. She kneels down and digs her hands deep into the earth, planting each seed with care. "Grow strong little seed, send out your roots, sprout your leader, and when the time is right, blossom and be fruitful," she says to herself. She hears a rustle in the grass and looks up. A sheep is walking toward her. *Hmmm! This sheep doesn't look like those in the neighbor's flock.*

"Hello there. Where did you come from?" Leda asks the sheep.

"I'm trying to find my way home. I saw a light from your farmhouse last night and thought this might be a safe place," the sheep says.

"Well, you've come to the right spot. What's your name?"

"Hugh."

"What a lovely and noble name. Do you know it means heart, mind, or spirit—the places where leadership begin?" she asks.

"No," he says.

"Here on the Leadership Farm, everything has purpose and meaning," says Leda. "We have many unique farm animals and plant the usual gardens and crops, but we also plant and grow special Leadership Gardens."

"What are those," asks Hugh, looking around, "and where are they?"

"They're not in this garden, but in your body, mind, heart, and spirit. Tending your Leadership Garden is the way you grow your leader and express your purpose and aim."

"That sounds a little strange."

"It is, for those who don't know that they have a leader hidden inside. What are you looking for Hugh?" asks Leda.

"I'm not sure," he says. "When I was a lamb, I played in a field with goats. One day, the farmer's son called me stupid and said I didn't belong in his field. That hurt my feelings."

"What did you do?" asks Leda.

"I ran home to ask my mother if I was stupid to play with goats. She said I wasn't and there was nothing wrong with playing with goats. She said all animals are unique and have something special to offer."

"It sounds like you have a wise mother."

"I did," says Hugh.

"What do you mean, you did?"

"One day I saw a pack of coyotes heading into our field. I tried to warn my mother but before I could reach her, the coyotes circled her. I knew she was in trouble, but I got scared and ran away."

"You didn't go back?"

"I was sure the flock wouldn't want a coward like me. So I left and I've been wandering ever since."

"Everyone feels frightened at times. It's natural when something like that happens; it's a survival response. But what happened to your mother?" Leda asks.

"I don't know."

"Then you don't know if the coyotes got her or if the flock has rejected you."

"You mean my mother could still be alive?" he asks.

"It's possible. And it's also possible that the flock might not reject you and could very well miss you."

"I doubt they would miss a coward like me."

"That isn't the truth – that's something you made up. Sit down beside me. I think you're ready to learn the first lesson on the farm." Leda puts down her trowel and smiles at Hugh.

LEADERSHIP GARDEN LESSON:

Leaders grow, they are not made.

— Peter Drucker

We begin with the Leadership Garden metaphor. Life begins as a seed that grows roots and a leader that has the potential to sprout personal greatness. Roots grow from our family and our own life experiences. In gardening, the leader is the stem – the primary shoot of a plant that will eventually produce flowers or fruits. Our leader is our mind, heart, and spirit. Like plants, each person is a leader waiting to sprout. Once blossomed, the leader inside re-sows the seeds of greatness and distributes them in the gardens of others.

Our body is the soil of our Leadership Garden, where the heart, mind, and spirit grow. The mind creates thoughts, the logic and reasoning we use to interpret the world. Our heart elicits physical responses to feelings, emotions, and passion. Our spirit nurtures the values, conscience, attitudes, and principles that provoke our thoughts, actions, and purpose.

The root of the word "leadership" is lead, which means to guide and direct. Our leader guides and directs our life and the actions we take that convey our leadership. To grow a Leadership Garden, the heart, mind, and spirit connect to plant and nurture the seeds of our best purpose and aim. Without purpose and aim, weeds can overrun our life and our Leadership Garden will wither and die.

In Leadership Gardens, two different conditions affect the growth of a leader. A survival condition promotes the growth of weeds, tenacious plants with deep taproots. These weeds diminish personal power and enable gossip, blame, and victimization. A thriving condition allows a leader vigorous, flourishing, and expansive growth, rooted in a strong mesh-like network of understanding, nurturing, inventive, quality, and unstoppable expression of leadership.

We cannot always control the circumstances of our lives, but we can always choose how we respond to them. When we want to thrive, rather than survive, we choose to pull our weeds and plant new seeds that empower us.

My family kept secrets and projected an image far different from the reality in our home. My father's drinking problem and my mother's bouts of depression led me to plant the weed of shame in my garden, choking out my leader. As an adult, I had been promoting the survival condition of my family in my personal and professional life. When I realized this, I chose to take responsibility, pulled that weed, and planted my Leadership Garden to thrive.

My first test of taking responsibility and choosing to thrive was right before I married my new husband, Terry. It had been a stressful time for both of us, working full-time, remodeling his home, selling my house, planning our wedding, and preparing for our first blended-family vacation. There were time pressures and I had begun to worry about finances.

One day, while working on Terry's house, we took a lunch break and began to discuss the expenses for our houseboat vacation. We both wanted our relationship to thrive but we had different communication and parenting styles. I suggested our children, who were young adults and teenagers, pay for the ski boat gas since they would use it most often. He disagreed, since we were the ones who had offered to take them on vacation.

"When are you going to make them grow up and take responsibility to help with family vacations?" I said.

Terry glared at me, said nothing, and walked away.

I followed him outside. "If this is how you are going to be when we don't agree, how we will ever survive?"

I left Terry's house upset and went home to the solace of my garden. I looked at my neglected flower beds and began to pull the weeds. Then I remembered something Terry had told me when we first met: "Our relationship is like the four seasons. How we weather each season and blend our families, will determine our strength and growth as a couple."

I was unaware I had gone into my old survival condition until our communication differences collided. I realized my accusatory statement had been unwarranted and I had been stubborn, just like the weeds in my garden, and I had grown persistent about my point of view. I knew in my heart that if I left Terry now it would destroy the special garden we had been cultivating.

I began to think about everything I loved about him. My mind calmed, my spirit lifted, and my garden was soon weed-free. I picked a bouquet of roses, put them in a vase, and took a shower.

When I went back to Terry's house with love in my heart, I was ready to work through our differences. I placed the roses on the patio table and we watched a beautiful sunset together. In that twilight moment, we vowed that we would never let anything that had the potential to be a weed, grow in our garden again. Since then, our relationship has flourished and our family has grown stronger with each new season.

Back in the garden, Leda stands, brushes off her knees, and begins to talk with Hugh about his Leadership Garden.

"You got scared, ran away, and decided you were a coward that day in the field. You could have told yourself that you were brave to get away safely or you could have gone back, yet you did neither," she says. "Can you see that your thoughts and reactions created a survival condition that changed your future?"

Hugh hesitates for a moment. "I guess so, but what do you mean, changed my future?"

"When you didn't go back, you changed your future into one of wandering alone. Today you decided to come here. That too, will change your future," Leda says. "But first it's important to learn that you have a choice about your garden condition. Try choosing courage and see how that feels."

"Okay, that makes a lot of sense," he says. "But I have two questions. Why did you say I made up being a coward and how can planting courage change the condition of my garden?"

"You will find the answer to both your questions here on the Leadership Farm. For now, do you think you understand the moral of this lesson?"

"I think so. The condition of my garden determines how it grows?" he asks.

"That's correct," Leda says, a smile on her face.

LEADERSHIP GARDEN EXERCISE ONE:

1. Find a notebook, pad of paper, or blank journal and title it, "My Leadership Garden Guidebook" to use for the exercises. On the top of the first page write, "What I Want in My Life." Make a list of *at least* three things that you currently don't have but want. It could be something you want to do, obtain, or experience as a feeling that relates to any area of your life.

2. On the top of the second page, write, "What I Don't Want in My Life." Make a list of *at least* three things that you currently have that you don't want. Again, it could be something you do, have, or experience as a feeling that relates to any area of your life.

3. Now pick a difficult relationship or situation where you used survival leadership or walked away. Describe it on the top of the next page.

4. Below that, state your thoughts regarding that relationship or situation. Some examples to get you started are:

- *I'm too. . .*
- *If only . . .*
- *They don't . . .*
- *I can't . . .*
- *They are . . .*

- *I should . . .*
- *They won't . . .*
- *I'm not . . .*
- *They shouldn't . . .*
- *It's not . . .*

5. Ask yourself if these statements empower your life and a thriving leadership condition. Write yes or no beside each statement. Cross out the "no" statements and circle the "yes" statements to use as a reminder for the next lesson.

Note: As you continue through the exercises, feel free to go back to the first two pages in your guidebook and add to the list of what you want or don't want in your life.

2

PLANTING A
LEADERSHIP
GARDEN

Reality germinates from the seeds

of early life experience. If those

seeds don't give us power, we can

choose to cultivate and replant

a new Leadership Garden.

— Debra J. Slover

THE SUN IS UP; Hugh and Leda sit in the cool shade of an old apple tree in the orchard. They begin to talk about planting his Leadership Garden. "Hugh, I'm glad you've chosen to plant the seed of courage," says Leda.

"Me too, but why did I plant the coward weed in my garden?" he asks.

"Because you were scared. Seeds are planted early in life by your reactions and responses to pleasant or unpleasant experiences. The decisions you make regarding those experiences and how you respond is often made without conscious thought. Sometimes those thoughts grow into weeds."

"I made up being a coward from something I thought?" asks Hugh.

"Yes, but you didn't know how your thoughts, feelings, and decisions would impact the growth of your Leadership Garden. These three things combined, guide and direct your behavior."

"Are you saying that I came here to learn how to lead my life?" he asks.

"Well," says Leda, "you did say you were trying to find your way home."

"What does that have to do with leadership?"

"You're the one leading your life, but you are going in a survival direction."

"So how do I go in a new direction?" he asks.

"You've already begun by choosing to plant the seed of courage. Up to this point, you've reacted to what happened and you got lost," she says. "It takes courage, Hugh, to be responsible for your life."

"But Leda, I don't know if I can go back," he says.

She picks up an apple blossom knocked down by yesterday's rain. "Look, this blossom would've become an apple, which reminds me of a quote by Arthur Miller: 'The apple cannot be stuck back on the tree of knowledge; once we begin to see, we are doomed and challenged to seek the strength to see more, not less.' Hugh, with your new knowledge, now that you know about your leader, you will be challenged."

Hugh lowers his head. "I've already had enough challenges in my life. Can't I just plant new seeds?"

"You can, but if you don't find the survival seeds that are growing into weeds," she says softly, "they will get in the way of your new direction. Let's look at how the brain works to understand this."

Hugh's eyes light up. "Are we going on a science field trip?"

"Just a brief one, into your garden."

PLANTING A LEADERSHIP GARDEN LESSON:

The first responsibility of a leader is to define reality.
— Max DePree

We begin this lesson with the assertion that we create our reality by the seeds we plant and nurture in our Leadership Garden. In Chapter One, we examined how the condition of our garden determines how our leader grows. Now we'll explore how that condition evolves from our view of reality.

Our unique genetic make-up influences how we interpret our environment, and that interpretation wires our brain, gives us the ability to function in the world, and creates our reality. It's human nature to seek what is pleasant and to avoid the unpleasant. We have a need to express ourselves, search for meaning in life, and protect ourselves from danger and threats. Pulling weeds enables us to thrive and re-sow seeds that will grant us the ability to experience our greatness—the essence of who we are.

To learn how to pull our weeds, let's look at the basic empowerment principle of Leadership Gardens, beginning with our mind. The elaborate mapping of the brain helps us learn from and respond to both pleasant and unpleasant life events.

Scientists previously thought the brain was hard-wired by genetics and early life experiences. Recently, scientists studying the brain discovered that we have the ability to rewire our brain in order to learn new things and create new experiences. In other words, our wiring is not fixed.

To help understand this, we'll look at the brain wiring process. It begins with a stimulus (seed) that comes into our body through one or more of our senses. We either notice or ignore the stimulus. If noticed, the stimulus is sent to our short-term memory. From there, we interpret and learn what is meaningful or useful and store it in one of our two long-term memory compartments for later retrieval.

Our explicit (conscious) memory stores the biographical events of our life, along with words, ideas, and concepts. Our implicit (nonconscious) memory stores procedural skills—like riding a bike or driving a car—and emotional conditioning from past events.[1]

When we receive a new stimulus, an impulse is sent to the heart and other organs that evoke feelings—pleasant, unpleasant, or neutral. The brain then calls up an emotional reaction that tells us how to respond to the stimuli. This all takes place simultaneously through nerve cells that fire neurotransmitters—chemical substances— across a synapse to other parts of our brain and body. Consequently, we learn by paying attention to our feelings and respond with both conscious thought and automatic emotional conditioning. This response completes the wiring process that creates our view of reality and the condition of our Leadership Garden.

---

[1] In my literature research, I found that neuroscientists use the term, "nonconscious," and psychologists use the term, "subconscious," to refer to the implicit memory. Regardless of the term, we are conscious but not aware. For simplicity, I'll use the commonly used term, "unconscious."

Intuition, often referred to as our sixth sense, is not connected to the sensory organs, per se, but it plays a key role in leadership, especially when it connects to our values, conscience, and purpose. Intuition is like a gut feeling or insight; there may not be any rational or tangible evidence to support or explain it, but we feel it as something real. If this feeling empowers us, we must pay attention; if not, we should ignore it.

Feelings and emotions also play a key role in the empowerment principle. We usually think of feelings and emotions as interchangeable and heart-centered, not mind-centered. Feelings are our body's response to emotions. Our emotions are evaluated and interpreted in the brain and reside in our long-term memory.

Stored in our long-term memory compartments are what psychologist's term, "corrective emotional experiences," (CEEs) for individuals, and, "collective emotional experiences," for groups. CEEs for groups are large-scale societal/historical events such as Pearl Harbor, September 11th, and Hurricane Katrina.

Whether in a group or as an individual, I'll call these experiences, "source events." Simply put, source events are experiences we cannot change. No matter how old we are when a source event occurs, it leaves its mark in our long-term memory compartments and, because of our unique wiring, no two people have the same emotional response to any one event.

Source events are neutral and have no power. The power lies in how our long-term memory is wired. Our emotional conditioning evokes an automatic reaction and then a response. Present and past events have no actual association, but the automatic reaction and response, triggered by a stimulus, may be the same. When the source event is retrieved by our conscious memory, it may cause us to relive an unpleasant experience with thoughts of, if only . . . I should have . . . why did . . . etc. These thoughts lead to regret, guilt, and dissatisfaction and reinforce the survival condition of our Leadership Gardens.

Since we now know that we have the ability to rewire our brain, here is the key to empowerment: CHOICE. Choice gives us the ability to choose our response to automatic emotional conditioning and to accept the things we cannot change.

A few years ago, Terry and I were watching the movie *A Beautiful Mind* at the local theater. At the point when John Nash was institutionalized, my stomach turned and I felt nauseated (feeling). Tears surfaced from deep inside (emotional reaction). I wanted to rescue John (response) and I was outraged at the twist in the plot (another emotion). Terry seemed to be enjoying the movie with no apparent adverse reaction. When he looked over at me and saw I was crying, he took my hand and asked if I wanted to leave. I shook my head (choice).

I recognized that I was having an emotional reaction to my mother's failed treatment (source event). I regained my composure, squeezed Terry's hand to let him know I was okay, and later, was glad that we had stayed to see the entire movie.

The memory of what happened with my mother is indelible. But I am comforted to know that the amazing ability of choice can heal the emotional scars of the past and create a new reality.

We each possess this power of choice, the empowerment key to our Leadership Garden. Not all source events are dramatic or unpleasant, even pleasant ones leave their mark in our long-term memory. Each time we choose to focus on the pleasant events of our life and not let the unpleasant ones dictate our response in a negative manner, we begin to rewire our brain and create a new reality.

Hugh and Leda walk back to the garden to review his lesson. Leda hears a familiar voice.

"I think Aristotle, my husband and Annabelle, our Border collie, are here," Leda says. She runs to her husband, kisses him on the cheek, and bends down to pet Annabelle. When she looks up, Hugh is hiding in the rose bushes outside the farmhouse gate.

"The roses look lovely, Leda, but why is a sheep hiding in them?" asks Aristotle.

"That's Hugh, he wandered onto our farm while I was planting the vegetable garden. He thinks he's a coward. I'm telling him about the Leadership Garden and helping him plant the seed of courage. We were just about to review the Planting a Leadership Garden lesson."

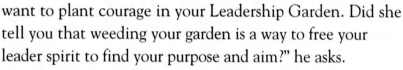

Aristotle walks over to Hugh and Annabelle scampers off to the barn.

"Leda tells me you want to plant courage in your Leadership Garden. Did she tell you that weeding your garden is a way to free your leader spirit to find your purpose and aim?" he asks.

Hugh backs away and moves toward Leda.

"I'm scared of Aristotle," he whispers to her.

"You don't need to be afraid. My husband is a strong but gentle man who would never hurt you."

"Leda, let me talk to Hugh for a moment," Aristotle says. "He may be responding to a source event."

"I won't harm you, Hugh, I love sheep," he says, smiling at Hugh. "Let's go back to what you learned earlier. You may be frightened of me because of a source event that happened in your past."

"When I heard your voice, it reminded me of how afraid I was when the farmer's son called me stupid and told me to get out of the field." Hugh says. "I thought you might make me leave."

"I certainly don't want you to leave, your leadership journey has just begun," says Aristotle. "Source events are like that. They remind you of something or someone from a past experience."

"I was afraid of you because you reminded me of the farmer's son?" Hugh asks.

"Possibly," says Aristotle. "But that was the past. You don't have to be scared now."

"I can see you are really nothing like the farmer's son."

"In Part Two of your journey, Annabelle will take you on the U.N.I.Q.U.E. tour of the farm where you will meet some of the other animals who live here," says Aristotle. "They'll teach you the rest of your lessons and Leda and I will meet up with you later."

Aristotle looks over at Leda. "Where's Annabelle?"

"I saw her head over to the barn," she says.

Aristotle pats his leg and calls out, "Annabelle, come here girl."

Annabelle runs out of the barn and into the garden, wagging her tail. "I had to tell my pups that I'm going to work and will be back later."

"You have pups?" Hugh asks. "Can I meet them?"

"Yes, after you've learned your lessons and completed the tour. For now, we have work to do," she says. "First, I'll take you to the Understanding Field to meet George the goat. He'll teach you about leader behaviors and how to balance them so you can thrive."

"I'd sure like that," says Hugh.

Aristotle and Leda walk toward the barn. Aristotle turns back to Hugh and says, "Now remember, you create your own reality, so create one that makes you strong."

"I will Aristotle. Sorry I was scared of you. From now on, I'll try to be strong," says Hugh.

"Hugh," says Leda. "Before you leave can you tell us the moral of this lesson?"

"I choose my reality?" he asks.

"Very good, though you sound unsure," she says.

"Well it is difficult to believe."

"You don't have to believe it, just think about it as you take your tour. You're in good hands with Annabelle."

"I can do that," he says and taps his hooves.

"Have a good time on your tour and enjoy all your new friends," says Aristotle. He takes Leda's hand and they wave good-bye and disappear into the barn.

PLANTING A LEADERSHIP GARDEN EXERCISE TWO:

1. In your guidebook, write down three recent experiences (or situations) that evoked a strong emotional reaction.
2. Next, identify your physical reaction (feelings) and your emotional response(s) to each experience.
3. See if there was a source event connected to each incident.
4. Identify whether the emotional response(s) and the action(s) you took was a weed or blossoming seed in your garden.
5. Now go back to the first exercise and see if any of the *if only . . . I should have. . . Why did . . .* statements are related to a source event that you can now choose to accept to empower yourself.

PART TWO

THE
U.N.I.Q.U.E.
TOUR BEGINS

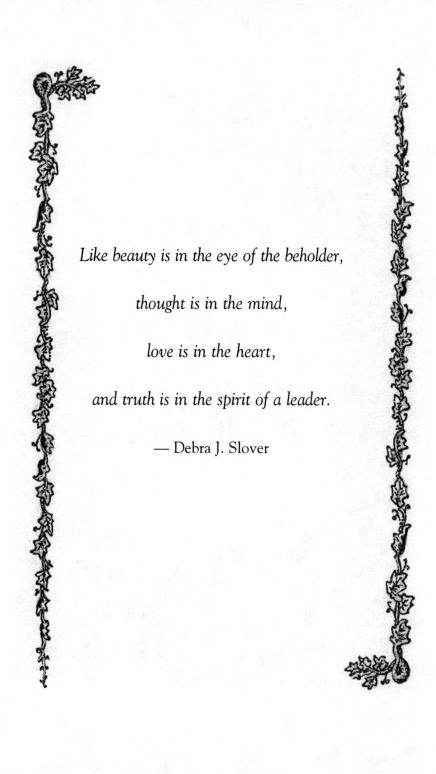

Like beauty is in the eye of the beholder,

thought is in the mind,

love is in the heart,

and truth is in the spirit of a leader.

— Debra J. Slover

Hugh and Annabelle talk for a few moments among the rose bushes.

"Annabelle, before we go, I have a question," says Hugh. "I noticed a wonderful fragrance in these bushes when I was hiding. What was that?"

"You smelled the roses; they do have a lovely aroma."

"There are so many. Do they have purpose and meaning too?" he asks.

"Of course, roses are a symbol of love."

"What does love have to do with leadership?"

"Aristotle and Leda planted this rose garden as a symbol of their love for each other and humanity. A leader can't thrive without love," says Annabelle.

"I was surprised when Leda told me that leadership was about how I guide and direct my life. I always thought it was about leading others to gain power and make things happen."

"Unfortunately, that's what many leaders think," says Annabelle. "Leda and Aristotle wanted to create a world that thrives with unique leadership expression and love is in the heart of all leaders. Power without love is force, and that's not leadership – that's control."

"If love is in my heart, is that where my leader comes from?" he asks.

"Not entirely. But love is what binds us together."

"What's going to happen on my U.N.I.Q.U.E. tour?" asks Hugh.

"You'll learn how to blend your heart, mind, and spirit to unearth your unique expression and connect with others. You'll discover the honor and privilege of leadership, and how it warms your heart and lifts your spirit when in service of another. A leader who thrives connects all three to see the favor, grace, and beauty of life."

Hugh pauses for a moment. "Annabelle, no one told me what your name means."

"It means favor, grace, and beauty."

He smiles. "No wonder you seem so wise."

"Thank you for the compliment," Annabelle replies. She looks up into the morning sun. "It looks like it's going to be a warm day. We'd better get started, there's a lot of Leadership Garden principles and practices for you to learn."

"What are those?"

"A Leadership Garden practice is the way you do something, kind of like a habit, and a principle is something that guides how you do it," she says. "In the Understanding Field, George the goat will show you how to balance, blend, and expand your leader behavior. Then we'll visit Blossom the cow in the Nurturing Meadow, where you'll learn leader-friendly gardening practices that keep your garden thriving."

"Sounds like I'm going to meet several new animals who have plenty to teach me," he says.

"That's not all. At the Inventive Roost, Robert the rooster will help you invent your purpose and aim and in the Quality Yard, Asli the goose will teach you leadership qualities and the attributes that are essential in all Leadership Gardens."

"Will I be done then?" he asks.

"No, next you'll meet Howard the horse at the Unstoppable Pasture, where you'll learn about commitment. And your last stop will be at the Expression Pen, where Allegra the pig will show you how to communicate your purpose and aim. It's like singing your unique leadership song."

"I'm going to learn how to sing too?"

"In a way," she says smiling. "You'll understand when we get there."

"This tour sounds like it's going to be fun. I hope I can remember everything," he says.

"Just take each lesson as it comes. The tour is intended to give you the tools you need to unearth your unique leader spirit," says Annabelle. "Now let's get going."

3

UNDERSTANDING
FIELD

We are the natural cultivators

of our Leadership Garden to

balance, blend, and expand

our behaviors to thrive.

— Debra J. Slover

I T'S MID MORNING WHEN Annabelle and Hugh arrive at the Understanding Field. George, a brindle colored goat, is under an oak tree on the far side of the field, munching on weeds.

Annabelle calls out, "George, come meet Hugh." Hugh furrows his brow. "What's wrong?"

"Annabelle, George's big horns and pointy beard reminds me of the billy goats back home," he says. "I sure hope he doesn't act like them."

"Don't worry," says Annabelle. "George knows how to behave. You can learn a lot from him."

"Hello Hugh. Welcome to the Understanding Field," says George. "I presume you're here to learn about leader behaviors."

"That's what Annabelle tells me," says Hugh.

"What do you know about leader behaviors?" asks George.

"Not much, except butting heads. My mom told me that kids butt heads to play, but adult goats do it to see who'll become the leader and dominate the herd. Is that what all leaders have to do?"

"Not in Leadership Gardens," says George. "When you understand how to cultivate leader behaviors, you'll realize that you don't have to butt heads with others to become a strong leader. I've not butted heads since I've been on the Leadership Farm."

"I don't want to do that either. What am I going to do in the Understanding Field?" asks Hugh.

"You will cultivate your I.Z.E."

"Is that dangerous?"

"No," George chuckles, "but it is quite revealing. Aristotle calls me a natural field cultivator because I enrich the soil so it can produce the plants we want to grow. And I eat the noxious weeds that stress the plants. Everything I eat is recycled as fertilizer and trampled into the ground while I graze. Just like I cultivate the field, you cultivate four leader behaviors that fertilize your garden. These behaviors are the Internal Zones of Expansion (I.Z.E.) that you'll use to cultivate your leadership."

"But how do I cultivate behavior?" asks Hugh.

"Well, your thoughts create the condition of your garden and fertilize your behavior. When your thoughts yield new behavior and a thriving condition, that makes you the natural cultivator of your garden," says George.

"How can I cultivate my new seed of courage?"

"By keeping your mind free of coward-like thoughts and fertilizing your behavior with thoughts of courage."

"That sounds like positive thinking," says Hugh.

Suddenly, Annabelle steps on a thistle, "OUCH!" She sits down to lick her paw. "You missed one, George. And Hugh, it's not only thinking positive but behaving positive."

George reaches down and eats the thistle. "Very tasty. Thanks for pointing that one out, Annabelle." He looks over at Hugh. "I think it's time to go to the Understanding Lesson to learn about cultivation and the four leader behaviors that will help grow your seed of courage."

UNDERSTANDING FIELD LESSON:

Leaders don't create followers, they create more leaders.
— Tom Peters

The next principle of a Leadership Garden is the cultivation of the behavior that will sprout our leader. Behavior is how we act, what we do, and who we think we are. When we cultivate our Leadership Garden, we fertilize four specific leader behaviors: visualize, organize, harmonize, and energize. The condition of our garden, our view of reality, and the survival or thriving tendencies of each behavior, determines how our garden grows. Tendencies, defined in this context, are frequent ways of behaving that take us in a certain direction and always produce the same result. Conscious and unconscious emotional conditioning frames our survival or thriving behavior tendencies.

Our dreams, aspirations, career goals, and/or relationships can become thwarted when we are unaware of the survival behavior tendencies we've established and the labels that we've placed on ourselves.

Behavior tendencies that encumber us I'll call, "spirit blockers." They seem fixed and unchangeable, but I have found that no behavior is fixed. Spirit blockers usually crop up when we are operating in a survival condition, allowing the repetition of a behavior that doesn't empower us. Thriving leaders take responsibility for everything that grows in their gardens, even weed-like survival behaviors.

So how do we actually alter our behavior to thrive? First, we need to let go of the notion that a particular behavior is fixed or is our true self. Then we look at the behaviors that block our spirit from thriving—this is where courage and choice come into play. It is not always easy to be responsible for our behavior in a survival condition, but when we are committed to thrive, the cultivation process becomes natural.

A spirit blocker I unearthed in my own garden popped up one day shortly after Terry and I had begun dating. Everything was going well, but I thought I should warn him about a tendency of mine that could cause problems in the future.

One afternoon over coffee, I said to Terry, "I want you to know that I can be intimidating sometimes."

"No you're not," he said.

"But you don't understand. Once you get to really know me . . ."

He put his hand over mine and asked, "Why do you want me to think that about you?"

My relationship with Terry was like a dream come true, but underneath I was terrified I would butt heads with him and ruin everything, as I had done in previous relationships. I thought that if I warned him in advance, it would head off any future disappointment for either of us. His question and refusal to agree with my belief empowered me to remove that spirit blocker. And dismissing the thought that I was intimidating was refreshing.

Terry and I eventually had a misunderstanding regarding the difference in our communication styles, but with my "intimidating" spirit blocker removed, I was willing to take responsibility for my behavior. We agreed to cultivate our relationship so it would grow strong and healthy, which gave me a new feeling of synergy—the combined action of two or more people creating a greater force than one.

Synergy is important in leadership and in gardening. Gardeners use the term synergy to define three or more units, common characteristics, colors, or textures of flowers or plants that create a unique garden design. The individual units alone are not a complete design, but when combined with others, they create an artistic whole that provides rhythm and balance. In Leadership Gardens, the synergy of the four behaviors gives us the design that makes our ideals, goals, and dreams come true.

Note: Pause and go to page 52 to complete the Leader Balance Inventory. Then follow the instructions to complete your Leader Balance Wheel on page 54. Resume reading when you have completed both.

The Leader Balance Wheel is a tool to help you cultivate, grow, and expand your Leadership Garden. Your Balance Wheel is always changing and most likely does not show the four behaviors equally balanced. No one behavior is better than the other is and should not to be used to stereotype yourself or others. Your highest score shows you how you view the world most often and your second highest score shows you how you accomplish tasks most often.

Now that you are aware of the unique synergy of your leader behavior, you will notice that visualize, organize, harmonize, and energize all denote action. You need all four to grow a strong and healthy Leadership Garden. When you understand the survival and thriving tendencies of each behavior, and how to cultivate them, your garden will blossom.

A thriving leader guides or directs at the appropriate times. Visualizing and organizing are direction-oriented behaviors; harmonizing and energizing are guidance-oriented behaviors. Following are the thriving tendencies of each behavior:

- Visualize is abstract in nature and grows thoughts, inspiration, imagination, ideas, and vision for purpose and aim.
- Organize is concrete in nature and grows methodology, order, and structure to fulfill goals.
- Harmonize is symbolic in nature and grows attunement, coordination, unity, and peace with inner self and others.
- Energize is literal in nature and grows play, vitality, strength, and joy for the adventure of life.

The survival tendencies of each behavior can be a source of dissatisfaction when working with others. They tend to surface as emotional reactions, mostly when under stress, and act like weeds to uproot the full potential of the behavior. Below are the survival tendencies of each behavior:

- Visualize grows dissatisfaction, self-centeredness, skepticism, difficulty, irritation, frustration, and feelings of being overwhelmed.
- Organize grows demands, criticism, self-righteousness, insensitivity, negativity, and control.
- Harmonize grows impracticality, defensiveness, drama, sensitivity, disagreeableness, distrust, and the need to withdraw.
- Energize grows reactivity, impatience, inconsideration, frustration, disruptiveness, anger, cynicism, and impulsiveness.

When looking at your Balance Wheel, you will notice that all of these behaviors are growing to some degree. When purpose and aim guide your leader and direct your behavior, you will nurture, blend, and balance all four behaviors to thrive and unearth the true leader within. You will learn to work well with others, pull weeds, and remove spirit blockers in your garden and support others to do the same.

A key element of all behavior is emotion. A prolonged emotional state often turns into a mood that affects our behavior and those around us. When a leader becomes moody, rigid, or stagnant, progress stops, emotions run high, and what is possible to achieve as an individual or in a group is compromised. Emotional conditioning, in reaction to source events, also plays a key role in these leader behaviors. The good news and bad news is that our emotions and moods are contagious and displayed in our behavior.

Now that we've looked at the thriving and survival tendencies of each behavior, we'll look at how these behaviors challenge leaders in making goals and dreams a reality.

- Visualize—the challenge is having ideas, dreams, and visions that make sense to others become reality. Staying on task or completing a project before beginning a new one can result in repeated failure and leaves others confused, overwhelmed, diminished, and annoyed.

- Organize—the challenge is to expand thinking beyond the facts that pose as reality by discounting ideas that can't be proven. Producing a tangible result, to the exclusion of new ideas, can stifle positive personal interaction and the creativity of others.
- Harmonize—the challenge is not to take the words and actions of others personally and to speak out or stand up for ideas that can make a valuable contribution when facing disagreement.
- Energize—the challenge is to play inside of conventional structures and rules. Impatience with process and the desire to avoid routine and boredom can have a negative impact on a group process.

My challenges as a thriving leader come from two strong direction-oriented behaviors that I had learned growing up: visualize and organize. When I was young, I was always on guard to protect myself; I felt a need to maintain control at all times. But my need to control frustrated me and I felt guilty about not being able to change. That continued throughout most of my life, until Terry refused to accept my thought that I could be intimidating. With that spirit blocker gone, my harmonize and energize guidance-oriented behaviors began to flourish.

This year, over a lovely Mother's Day dinner, I told my children how much I had learned and grown since the last Mother's Day I shared with my own mom, 30 years ago. My daughter put down her fork and looked at her new sister-in-law. "Yeah, Mom is not the same person since she met Terry. She used to intimidate our friends until they got to know her." Her comment made me laugh and warmed my heart, knowing that I had learned to balance my leader behaviors.

People will only take so much direction before their leader balance and creativity becomes compromised. When I allow others to be themselves, without trying to fix or change them, and focus on their positive behaviors, extraordinary results show up. If that's not happening, I know it's time to cultivate and weed my garden.

So far, we've learned that free will allows us to choose the condition of our garden and define our reality. Now we can choose to balance and blend these behaviors to expand our own leadership and our ability to work well with others. Understanding the survival and thriving tendencies and the challenges of each leader behavior gives us the power to be the natural cultivator of our garden, moving us one step closer to our unique leadership expression with purpose and aim.

———————

Let's return to the Understanding Field to see what Hugh has learned.

George and Annabelle have almost reached the oak tree. Annabelle looks back at Hugh, shuffling behind, his Leader Balance Wheel in his mouth. "Notice how Hugh drags his feet and the look on his face when he appears to be deep in thought," she says to George.

Suddenly, Hugh stumbles on a small branch. His knees buckle but he manages to catch his balance. "Nice save, Hugh," says George, rubbing his neck on the fence post. "Stick your Balance Wheel on this nail. What did you find out about yourself in the Understanding Field Lesson?"

"I learned that I should eliminate the thought that 'I am a coward' from my Leadership Garden. It makes me scared, sad, and lonely and now I see I'm the only one who can change that. And I also learned I should watch where I'm going and pick up my feet."

"You listened and learned well," says Annabelle.

George removes the branch from his path and puts it under the tree. "I'll munch on that later," he says. "It reminds me of a legend that said wands made of oak help us get in touch with strength and inner power. Hugh, your Balance Wheel helps you find the inner power, courage, and strength to be flexible and to balance the rigid thoughts and behavior that don't grow your leader."

"I like that idea," says Hugh, "but I am not clear about one thing."

"What's that?"

"Are all spirit blockers weeds?"

"Yes, but not all weeds are spirit blockers," says George.

"I'm confused," says Hugh.

"Think of it this way. A spirit blocker is a thought that doesn't empower you. Some behavioral tendencies are like weeds that pop up now and again, but they're only how you reacted emotionally and then responded at the time," says George. "The thought that you were a coward stuck with you as the truth and became a spirit blocker."

"Then not all of the things I believe about me are spirit blockers?"

"That's right. Some truths give you inner power, and those are the ones to nurture," says George.

Hugh looks down at the ground. "What if someone else calls me a coward?" he mutters to Annabelle.

"Sometimes what others say about you may give you an insight into the weed-like behaviors or spirit blockers you can't see," she says. "If what others say doesn't help your leader to grow, don't make it your truth."

George walks over to the fence post. "Let's look at your Balance Wheel to help you understand," says George. "Hmmm. You harmonize and energize most often and the behaviors you want to fertilize are organize and visualize."

"What does that mean?" asks Hugh.

"It may mean that you love people and are playful. When people or situations are unpleasant, you back away and that makes you feel like a coward," George says. "Hugh, you've planted courage to face conflict and can now choose when to back away. A thriving leader cultivates and nurtures all four behaviors with purpose and aim."

"When do I find my purpose and aim?" asks Hugh.

"Be patient. Remember, impatience is one of the survival tendencies of energize behavior," says Annabelle.

"How can I be patient when I am so anxious to know my purpose?"

"Cultivating and growing your garden takes time and patience and is a mark of a good gardener," says George. "Now it's time for Blossom the cow to teach you some practices that are necessary to grow your garden. Then you will get to invent your purpose and aim. In the meantime, harmonize is flourishing on your Balance Wheel. You can use it to counterbalance your impatient energize behavior."

"It's exciting to know that something is flourishing in my garden." Hugh pauses and looks out at the field. "Is there anything else I should know before I leave here?" he asks.

"Leaders who depend upon past survival behavior, create a crooked path. Those who look too far ahead may fail to see what's right in front of them and stumble," says George.

"I'm not sure I understand," says Hugh.

Annabelle replies, "When you let spirit blockers and other weeds get in your way, you lose the opportunity to grow and thrive, limiting what you see, where you step, and the path you take in life."

"I like the idea of choosing my own path," says Hugh. "So, even though I have some survival tendencies, and stumble once in a while, I can still grow my Leadership Garden to thrive?"

"Absolutely," says George. "Just unblock your spirit, cultivate your I.Z.E., and follow your dreams."

"Speaking of paths, can you tell us the moral of this lesson before we proceed?" asks Annabelle.

"I am the cultivator of my garden to balance, blend, and expand my leader behaviors. And learn to be patient. Right, George?"

"Excellent recall," he replies. "And yes, Hugh, patience is necessary to be a good leader."

"By George, I think he's got it," jokes Annabelle.

Hugh and Annabelle smile and nod goodbye to George.

"Don't forget your Leader Balance Wheel to show Blossom," says Annabelle. Hugh takes his Balance Wheel off the nail and they head straight to the Nurturing Meadow.

UNDERSTANDING FIELD
EXERCISES THREE—A AND B:

Exercise A—Spirit Blockers: On the top sheet of a blank page in your guidebook draw four columns and title them Truths, Age, Feeling, and How Long. See sample below:

TRUTHS	AGE	FEELING	HOW LONG
I'm bold	16	Powerful—S	37 years
I'm not good enough	5	Scared—W	48 years

1. In the "Truths" column, list everything you think about yourself that is true (i.e. I am shy, attractive, unlovable, outgoing, difficult, bold, courageous, vivacious, etc.).
2. In the "Age" column write down how old you were when you first realized your truths. Think about the source event that instigated that feeling.
3. In the "Feeling" column, describe the feeling you have about your truths. Place an S for seed or W for weed next to each feeling.
4. Subtract the age in the middle column from your current age and place that number in the "How Long" column. This is the number of years you have believed this truth about yourself. You may find it hard to give up some of your spirit blockers, depending upon how long you have

held on to them. But remember, if it doesn't empower you, it may be time to weed it from your garden.

5. If you haven't completed your Leader Balance Inventory and Balance Wheel, do so now.

6. Following your Spirit Blocker Exercise, make a list of survival tendencies from the four leader behaviors you experience most often from the bulleted list on the bottom of page 43. Use this list as a reminder of when it's time to cultivate and weed your garden.

7. You could also ask your friends, family, or co-workers to complete the Inventory using their feelings about how they perceive you. You can use their tallies to compare how you perceive yourself versus how others see you.

Exercise B[2]—Leader Balance Inventory and Leader Balance Wheel:

Leader Balance Inventory

Step One—Read across each row on page 53. Use each number from the rating scale below only once in each row.

Rating Scale: 4 = most like you; 3 = somewhat like you; 2 = somewhat least like you; 1 = least like you. A sample looks like this:

| Row 1 | 4 Problem solver | 1 Sensible & logical | 2 Good listener | 3 Negotiator |

---

[2] **Exercise B Disclaimer:** This exercise is not a psychological profile, nor scientifically validated and is only an indicator of how you responded to the inventory at this particular time.

	Column 1	Column 2	Column 3	Column 4
Row 1	4 Problem solver	3 Sensible & logical	2 Good listener	1 Negotiator
Row 2	4 Creative	1 Structured	2 Adaptable	3 Spontaneous
Row 3	4 Competent	1 Loyal	3 Appreciative	2 Playful
Row 4	4 Set the rules	2 Enforce the rules	3 Obey the rules	1 Avoid the rules
Row 5	4 Pacesetter	2 Decision Maker	1 Supporter	3 Competitor
Row 6	4 Ideas	3 Process	1 Feelings	2 Action
Row 7	1 Dreamer	3 Practical	2 Understanding	4 Casual
Row 8	3 Asks "Why"	4 Asks "How"	1 Asks "Who"	2 Asks "What"
Row 9	2 Change	3 Results	1 Values	4 Freedom
Row 10	4 Build upon	3 Count on	2 Depend upon	1 Bet on
Row 11	4 Says "I think"	1 Says "I should"	2 Says "I feel"	3 Says "I know"
Row 12	4 Initiative	3 Direction	1 Guidance	2 Adventure
	42 Total	29 Total	21 Total	28 Total

Step Two—Add up the total in each column.

Step Three—Take the total score from each column and enter it on the line next to the corresponding column number on the Leader Balance Wheel on page 54. For example, enter the Column 1 score on the Visualize Column 1 Score line. Then color in your score on each quadrant of the Balance Wheel to get a visual picture of your current leader balance.

Leader Balance Wheel

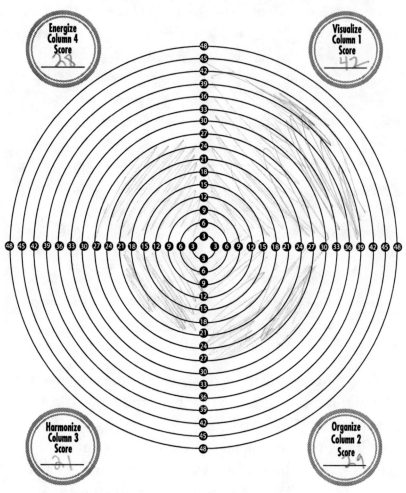

4

NURTURING
MEADOW

True leaders nurture their own

and other's Leadership Gardens

to sprout greatness.

— Debra J. Slover

HUGH AND ANNABELLE ARRIVE at the Nurturing Meadow around noon; wildflowers and tall fescue wave in the breeze. Blossom is grazing next to a barbed wire fence entwined with red and white roses. The sun shimmers on her black and white hide.

"Annabelle, there's a mark on Blossom's shoulder that looks like a flower," Hugh says.

"Blossom was born with a spot that looks like an anemone, a wildflower that blooms here in the meadow. That's why Leda and Aristotle named her Blossom."

"Does that flower have a meaning too?" he asks.

"Yes, the anemone symbolizes the concept of being forsaken. Forsake means to give up a habit or way of life," says Annabelle, "and now that you realize how sad and lonely you were, you can abandon that life and the old behaviors that don't grow your leader."

When they get closer to Blossom, she looks up and, true to her name, gives her visitors a beautiful flowering smile.

"Hello Annabelle, who is this adorable fellow with you?" she asks.

"This is Hugh," Annabelle says, "we just left George in the Understanding Field."

"Wonderful. Hugh, I see you have your Leader Balance Wheel," says Blossom, "let's take a look." She studies it for a moment and then looks up at Hugh. "Seems like you care a lot about peace, unity, fun, and play."

"Oh yes!" says Hugh. "One of my favorite pastimes when I was growing up was playing with the other animals on the farm. But I didn't like the billy goats butting heads or the farmer's kids picking on us. George helped me understand I didn't like those actions because they went against my harmonize leader behavior."

"Very good," says Blossom. "Now that you've learned about the four leader behaviors and the thriving and survival tendencies of each, we'll look at what can nurture or stunt the growth of your Leadership Garden. This will help you use thriving leader behaviors."

"You mean there's more than planting seeds, pulling weeds, and cultivating my garden?"

"Absolutely! You need to nurture your garden along with others and not do anything that would stunt their growth."

"Why should I care about someone else's garden?" he asks.

"Your garden won't thrive alone or in isolation," Blossom says.

"It won't?"

"No. That's working against nature and that doesn't sprout greatness in the world," says Annabelle. "We are all interdependent upon each other and our environment and how you tend your garden can influence others."

"I see," says Hugh.

Blossom nods toward the fence. "Let's look at the relationship between Leadership Gardens and my rose bushes," says Blossom. "Roses are my favorite flower and Aristotle and Leda helped me plant them."

"How do you take care of so many rose bushes?" he asks.

"I get help from Leda and Aristotle and the others on the farm. The biggest chore is to protect the rose bushes against blight, a disease that thwarts their growth." Blossom points to the rose leaves. "This powdery mildew is causing this young leaf to curl and turn purple. The stem is starting to distort and dwarf and if I don't treat it soon, the new rosebud may wither and the entire rose bush could die."

"That sounds pretty serious," says Hugh.

"It is and I need to take action before the winds come. If the mildew spores blow on to the other young leaves, the infection will spread."

"How do you stop it?"

"I remove the damaged leaves and apply an eco-friendly fungicide that doesn't harm other plant and animal life, and ultimately our planet Earth," says Blossom. "I also deadhead the spent flowers to encourage growth of new buds."

Annabelle says, "To thrive, Hugh, you need to follow 'leader-friendly gardening practices too.'"

"What are those?" he asks.

Blossom replies, "They're personal and socially responsible practices, such as being kind to others and being responsible for what is growing and wilting in your garden."

"Using these practices makes you a leader-friendly gardener," says Annabelle.

"Next we'll go to the Nurturing Meadow lesson to learn more about those practices," says Blossom.

"Good," says Hugh. "I don't want blight in my Leadership Garden."

NURTURING MEADOW LESSON:

If you judge people, you have no time to love them.
— Mother Teresa

So far, we have talked mostly about Leadership Garden principles. Now we'll focus on practices that are necessary to grow a thriving Leadership Garden. The following six leader-friendly gardening practices open our hearts, bind us together, and lift our spirits:

- Be nonjudgmental
- Use empathy
- Eliminate blame
- Don't enable
- Prune gossip
- Eradicate victimization

We begin with the first three practices. Forcing our opinions or personal values on others is toxic to our garden. Being judgmental separates us from others and robs us of love and appreciation. Suspending judgment by separating the behavior from the person, allows loving thoughts and communication about acceptable and unacceptable behaviors, without being self-righteous and enabling. This requires skill in speaking and listening to others and that skill begins with empathy—the ability to listen to another's thoughts, feelings, and opinions.

To practice empathy, we need to be responsible for our own thoughts and feelings, suspend judgment, and give up "being right" for the moment. In the heat of an argument this may be difficult, especially when we have strong beliefs or a message we feel is important to convey. Suspending judgment of another, not always "being right," and really listening, works wonders.

Empathy is a bridge from survival to thriving leadership and is a powerful way to interact with others. This subtle shift in thinking is strong fertilizer for Leadership Gardens. The more open and receptive we are to others, the more open and receptive they are to us. Remember, emotions and moods are contagious and are at the root of much social friction.

Judgmental and enabling behaviors have the potential to destroy many personal, family, and professional relationships and thwart organizational, religious, environmental, and governmental missions. If you think about it, most wars and battles fought throughout history have been over personal, moral, religious, or political points of view. Imagine a world where empathy is the norm and leadership thrives. The good news—it starts with us.

Here's an illustration of the importance of these three practices. In the early eighties, I was hired to develop a leadership approach for the youth traffic safety program at Oregon State University. No one but my supervisor knew that my ex-husband, who had numerous drunk driving offenses, and I had completed a treatment program for his alcoholism. We learned a lot and the program helped us get to the root cause of his alcoholism and my enabling behavior.

But at work, I faced the dilemma of how to prevent teens from driving impaired without addressing teen drinking and enabling behavior. With a husband in recovery, I feared the judgment of others and that speaking out about my personal life would damage my family and ruin my professional credibility. However, as an educator with first-hand experience of alcoholism, I was determined to prevent substance abuse in my own children and the youth I served. I needed to take a nonjudgmental, but empathic approach that did not enable unsafe and unhealthy behavior.

We named our program Oregon Student Safety On the Move (OSSOM). Our focus would be promoting personal responsibility and legal, safe, and healthy behavior. The sense of being in control of our lives would be the key. The challenge was to take the right or wrong judgments out of our interactions and replace them with personal and social responsibility, love, and compassion. My students and I took great care to separate the person from their behavior and tried to make a difference in a nonjudgmental and proactive way that didn't damage our relationships or enable undesired behavior.

Throughout that time, I was unaware that the shame about my personal life had enabled my own survival behavior. Only many years later would I learn the real impact of keeping that secret.

The fourth leader-friendly gardening practice is to prune gossip. Expressing a negative opinion about someone in his or her absence is unkind. On the surface, it seems like a harmless form of entertainment, due to a lack of anything better to talk about. Unfortunately, talking about the faults or misfortunes of others makes some people feel better about their own life. A malicious character attack is similar to the destruction of our own and another's garden, but the true underbelly of gossip is that it diminishes personal power and trust with others. A thriving leader does not engage in or tolerate gossip and prunes it when it begins.

The fifth practice is to eliminate blame—holding others responsible or at fault for something that we chose to participate in. Blame is a more severe form of gossip and a way to deflect personal responsibility. Taking 100% responsibility for ourselves eliminates blame and gives us personal power.

The sixth and most serious infection in a Leadership Garden is victimization. Blame and victimization often go hand in hand and can be devastating to a leader. Victimization is an unfortunate cultural phenomenon that is pervasive in today's society and takes the attention away from those who are the true victims. Victims need support to heal and restore their power, not be rendered helpless and diminished, leaving them even more victimized. Victimization is a form of survival leadership that robs us of the opportunity to be in control of, and responsible for, how we experience life.

The following are victim-like behaviors that infect Leadership Gardens:

- Blaming others
- Being morally right and making others wrong
- Shirking responsibility
- Feeling entitled to sympathy because of our misfortunes
- Righteous indignation for being wronged

Before I met Terry, I realized I had been living my life as a victim. I was going through a divorce and I knew something had to change. A colleague recommended a three-day course on how to live with power, freedom, and full self-expression. I took his suggestion and I went into the weekend looking for tips and techniques on how to change my life. What I got was the realization that my secret and shame had enabled me to be, at times, irresponsible and powerless in both my professional and personal life.

It was so simple, there was nothing to change except learning to be responsible for my experience and view of life. From the vantage point of not being a victim, I began to see my life differently; my inner power emerged and the freedom to express myself came alive.

Then I met Terry on a camping trip. I had already formed an opinion about him based on what I had heard from others. The first night, sitting around the campfire, we were two single people in our mid-forties who had nothing in common except children and divorces. We watched the fire and began to share our divorce war stories (gossip). I decided to defer my judgment and listen to him.

Somewhere in the course of our conversation, the topic shifted from what our ex-spouses did (blame), to how we felt (victims). When I saw myself through Terry's story, I shifted from being a victim to taking responsibility. It was like having a heart-to-heart conversation with my ex-husband about what it must have been like for him to live with me. When I spoke about my life, Terry saw the same thing. For the first time, we saw ourselves through the eyes of our ex-spouses (empathy).

We talked about what it would be like for our children if we took responsibility for our part in our respective divorces, rather than continuing to blame our ex-spouses. We knew of cases where blame and victimization had remained years after a divorce and neither of us wanted that.

By sharing our stories with an eye toward empathy, and taking responsibility for our failed marriages, Terry and I became friends, fell in love, and later became husband and wife. Today we have a loving, blended, and thriving family Leadership Garden.

———————

Back in the Nurturing Meadow, Blossom looks over at Hugh, shuffling his hooves. "Why's he doing that?" she asks Annabelle.

"He seems to do that when he's deep in thought and a little uncomfortable," she whispers back. Annabelle walks over to Hugh and puts her paw on his shoulder. "Hugh, you look worried."

"I think that nurturing the seed of courage is going to take a lot of work," he says.

"Why do you say that?" asks Blossom.

"Because I don't know I if I can ever overcome running from conflict and danger."

"That's your emotional conditioning talking like a victim, not you," says Blossom. "Besides, there's nothing wrong with you. When you take responsibility for your life, you begin to realize that you can choose fear or courage at any time."

"That sounds easier said than done," he says.

"Being responsible takes practice and commitment," says Annabelle. "You'll learn more about that a little later."

"For now," says Blossom, "let's make sure you understand leader-friendly gardening practices."

"But Blossom, how do I keep from becoming a victim when there is so much I don't have control over, like those bad coyotes that attacked my mom?"

"On the farm, we don't believe in bad people or animals," Blossom says. "By nature, all people and animals are primarily concerned with survival. Coyotes are predatory animals and unfortunately, sheep and cattle are some of their prey. It's their nature but it doesn't make them bad."

"Why not?" Hugh asks.

"Coyotes are doing what they need to do to survive, but that's not the kind of survival we are talking about here on the farm," she says. "Some leaders become predatory in their quest for power or approval as a means of survival."

Annabelle nods. "It's natural to want control, as well as approval; it makes you feel good and powerful. But when you seek that at the expense of others, it becomes dangerous and harmful behavior."

"How do you avoid that?" asks Hugh.

"If someone hurts my feelings, I don't judge them, but I do tell them how their words or actions make me feel," Annabelle says. "I try to focus on their positive behavior and have empathy for them. I can also choose not to be around others who do and say hurtful things."

Blossom says, "If they're dangerous, I run like the wind, just like you ran from the coyotes."

"And I chase them away," says Annabelle. "Unfortunately, once you found safety, you kept on running instead of going back to find out what happened."

"But what if the coyotes killed my mom? Don't you think that's wrong?" he asks.

"It's not for me to judge," says Blossom. "I hope she's alive, but if she's not, you can't change that. And it doesn't mean you won't feel hurt, that's a natural response to any loss. Accepting a situation, without judgment, is a powerful leader-friendly gardening practice."

Annabelle asks, "Would you be willing to accept the fact that she might be gone without becoming a victim?"

"I didn't realize I was acting like a victim until this lesson."

"When you decided you were a coward and didn't go back to your flock, you became a victim and lost some personal power. But you didn't realize that at the time," says Blossom. "Now you know, if you want to thrive, you can't think of yourself as a victim."

"I want to thrive and not be a victim," says Hugh. "But I am still going to run from coyotes."

"And you should, because they pose real physical danger to us," says Blossom. "But instead of accepting the nature of the coyote and what happened, you're blaming and judging them for behavior they cannot change and yourself for a situation you cannot change."

"I'm not doing that," he says.

"Well, Hugh, you just did a few moments ago when you asked us to agree with you about the coyotes," says Annabelle. "Judging the coyote and blaming yourself for not being able to help your mom became part of your defense against feeling helpless and the emotional pain of possibly losing her."

"The point is, Hugh, when you accept a situation without judgment, you have the power to choose and be responsible for your experience," says Blossom. "When you resist the reality of a situation and fail to see it for what it is, you lose power, become a victim, and love disappears from your heart."

"So if I accept a situation for what it is, don't judge and blame others or myself, and take responsibility for my thoughts, feelings, and actions, I'll have love in my heart and thrive?" asks Hugh.

"Precisely," says Blossom. "Not only that, but you will have the ability to love others and see their greatness."

"WOW! That would be great," says Hugh.

Blossom smiles and says, "Now it is time for Annabelle to take you to the Inventive Roost to meet Robert. He'll help you invent your purpose and aim. Before you go, can you tell us the moral of this lesson?"

"I sure can," he says. "GREAT leaders blossom with love and empathy."

Blossom laughs. "You added great, but that works since you learned the lesson so well. Remember, to have love in your heart and thrive, you must forsake your negative past."

"Thank you, Blossom," Hugh says. "Annabelle, will I need my Balance Wheel again?"

"Yes, bring it along." Hugh and Annabelle wave goodbye to Blossom and dash off to the Inventive Roost.

NURTURING MEADOW EXERCISE FOUR:

1. On the next page of your guidebook, write down the name of someone with whom you have had differences.
2. List what you see in their behavior that you don't like. Now list what you see in your own behavior that you don't like. See which are similar. Often what we don't like about others, we don't like about ourselves. If this person is close to you, have them take the Leader Balance Inventory and complete the Balance Wheel to see where you are alike and dissimilar.

3. Let go of your defenses and be honest with yourself to see where judgments, gossip, blame, or victimization may be infecting your relationship. Determine which leader-friendly gardening practices you will use to alter your view of the relationship.
4. Now pick an unpleasant situation and go through the same process.

Note: I encourage you to come back to this exercise whenever you face a conflict to help determine if you are using leader-friendly gardening practices.

5

INVENTIVE
ROOST

PURPOSE

HATCH NEW WAYS OF BEING

NEW FOOD FOR THOUGHT

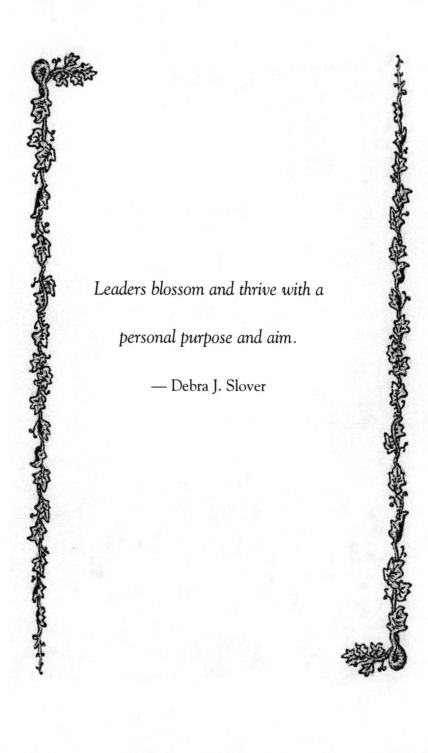

Leaders blossom and thrive with a

personal purpose and aim.

— Debra J. Slover

THE EARLY AFTERNOON SUN beats down on Annabelle and Hugh. They slow their pace and Annabelle gives Hugh some insight into his next lesson at Inventive Roost.

"We're almost to the Inventive Roost where you'll meet Robert the rooster. His job is to protect the hen house from predators like foxes and wolves. But he also shows leaders how to invent their personal purpose and aim," she says.

"Will my purpose help protect me from the coyotes?"

"No. Remember, that's physical danger. But it will help protect your future as a thriving leader. Up to this point, we have talked a lot about your past and present reality. Now you will begin to create a new reality and new experience, one that you choose."

Hugh and Annabelle find Robert on the corner fence post, his head tucked under his wing. When they approach, Robert opens an eye and points his bright red comb toward the sky. "Annabelle, who do ya' have there with ya'?" Robert crows, his wattle wiggling.

"This is Hugh. We just left Blossom in the Nurturing Meadow," says Annabelle.

"Fabulous," says Robert. "I see you have your Balance Wheel. So you're here to rule the roost?"

Hugh puts down his wheel. "No, I'm here to find my purpose and aim."

"That's what I said. You're here to invent your purpose and aim. To do so, you'll need to scramble who you A.R.E. and pluck your E.A.R.S. to rule the roost . . ."

Hugh leans over to Annabelle. "Is he serious?" he whispers.

"Yes, but scrambling who you are and plucking your ears isn't what you think. I forgot to mention that Robert's name means bright and fame. And every so often he thinks he's a famous orator," she says softly. "Sometimes he gets carried away with his analogies, but you can't help but love his enthusiasm."

Annabelle and Hugh giggle and Robert stretches his shiny blue, green, and black wings. Words continue to fly from his beak. ". . . to create your destiny, be master of your fate, shed new light on the world, and toot your own horn . . ."

"Robert!" shouts Annabelle.

Robert stops talking and looks over at them. "Pardon me for being so inspired by myself. Where did I lose you?" he asks.

"The part about scrambling and plucking," says Hugh.

"I see. I forgot to explain how I look at inventing your purpose."

"That would help," says Hugh.

Robert hops off the fence post. When he lands, his blonde cape feathers drape him like a king's robe. "Inventing your purpose starts with A.R.E.—A stands for actions, R stands for results, and E stands for experience. Your thoughts and feelings impact your actions, which gets ya' results in life."

"I thought I had to do something to be a leader and get results."

"That's what many leaders think," says Robert. "Everybody takes actions and get results, but you may not know that it's your thoughts and feelings that give you the experience of leadership."

"Robert, I thought experience was what I'd learned in the past."

"That's one way to look at it, but I'm talking about experience as a feeling. When you feel good about what you're doing and are grateful for what you have, you have the experience of being a leader."

"So what about plucking my ears?" Hugh asks.

"In the Inventive Roost, we scatter new food for thought and hatch new ways of being to pull out your leader within. E.A.R.S. is simply A.R.E. scrambled up with a letter S for synergy at the end."

"Do you recall the definition of synergy from the Understanding Field?" asks Annabelle.

"Yes," Hugh's ears perk up. "Synergy is a combination of behaviors that make up my unique leadership, like an artistic design with rhythm and balance. So is my purpose and aim kind of like my leadership omelet?"

"Shhhhh." Robert looks over at the hen house. "We don't mention that word around here. But verrrry good. You're going to make a great orator. Synergy in the Inventive Roost combines your feelings, thoughts, and behavior to invent your purpose and aim. It begins with the experience you want to have now."

"I'm not sure I understand," says Hugh.

"Hugh, your mind is programmed by your past experiences and you may be stuck there," says Annabelle. "The purpose you invent for yourself will guide your future and aim you in a new direction."

"That sounds like a great idea," says Hugh.

"It is," says Robert. "Invention lets you experiment with your E.A.R.S. and unlock your imagination to find out what inspires you. But first you need to let go of any truths that may still limit you."

"The truth again," Hugh lowers his eyes. "I already planted courage, eliminated the thought that I was a coward, and learned how to nurture my garden. Isn't that enough?"

"It's the beginning," replies Robert. "With purpose and aim, your future will no longer depend upon your past or current experiences. It will depend on what you invent as your true expression of leadership."

"But what if someone else has my purpose?" asks Hugh. "Will I be able to have that future too?"

"You bet," says Annabelle. "Even if someone else uses the same words, how you express your purpose and aim will always be unique to you."

Hugh grins and says, "I'm ready to learn how to scramble and pluck my E.A.R.S. Robert, where do I start?"

"In the Inventive Roost Lesson—of course," he replies.

INVENTIVE ROOST LESSON:

Efforts and courage are not enough
without purpose and direction.
— John F. Kennedy

In Chapter One, we learned that our spirit lies in the values, conscience, attitudes, and principles that provoke our thoughts, actions, and purpose. The next task in the Leadership Garden is to invent a purpose and aim, a phenomenon of unique self-expression that will allow our leader spirit to blossom. When we discover and express our purpose, leadership takes on new meaning.

When we are stuck in a pattern of trying to succeed in order to obtain happiness, satisfaction, and fulfillment, we often fail to see new opportunities and enjoy the experience of *being* a leader. A garden in survival condition, constantly eroded by automatic emotional reactions and responses, keeps us from inventing our purpose and expanding.

I found this to be true when I started my leadership consulting business and moved OSSOM into my home. The funding for OSSOM had ended and I was disheartened and lost; I couldn't seem to re-ignite my enthusiasm. For me, leadership was about the honor and privilege of *being* a person who makes a difference in the world. I had defined myself by what I did and how hard I worked, but it was never enough. My survival condition had robbed me of the true joy, satisfaction, and fulfillment of the experience of *being* a leader.

When I invented a personal purpose and aim to grow my leader within, I found the joy, satisfaction, and fulfillment I had been striving for. I began with the *experience* I desired, the *actions* I would take, and *results* I wanted.

On the following chart, I divided my experiences into two categories: inspiring and dispiriting. I looked at my experiences and saw that I had allowed myself to become resigned and sad. I knew I had a choice to be that way or not, so I chose the two most inspiring experiences: empowerment and extraordinary.

EXPERIENCES

INSPIRING	DISPIRITING
Happiness	Sadness
Connection	Loneliness
Peace	Anger
Courage	Fear
Boldness	Resignation
Brave	Coward
Strong	Weak
Power	Force
Empowerment	Helpless
Extraordinary	Ordinary
Freedom	Stuck
Love	Hate

Next, I created an actions chart (page 82) to look at what I enjoyed and what I avoided. My favorite action word was "leadership." The action I avoided most, "asking for help," made me chuckle. I wanted to contribute and make a difference, but I refused to ask for help because I feared it was a sign of weakness.

ACTIONS

ENJOY	AVOID
Creating charts and grids	Learning new stuff that seems hard
Organizing	Learning new computer programs
Gardening	Cleaning house
Playing with my grandchildren	Doing the laundry
Helping others	Being told no
Planning events	Asking for help
Flexible schedule	Working alone
Writing emails	Routine
Remodeling my home	Shopping, especially for shoes and groceries
Leadership	Making phone calls
Playing cribbage	Writing letters and grants
Making a difference	Reading a lot
Dreaming	

Then I created a results chart and listed my desires and needs. I realized my actual needs were few, compared to my desires, so I allowed myself to imagine my dreams and chose, "unstoppable." I realized I had let my fears stop me from achieving my most important goals and that left me feeling dissatisfied.

RESULTS

DESIRES	NEEDS
More time	Food
Relaxation	Sleep
Abundance	Energy
Fun	Satisfaction
Ease	Roof over my head
Joy	Connection to others
Mastery of skills	
Focus	
Clarity	
Certainty	
Unstoppable	
Dreams fulfilled	
Challenge	
Inner peace	

I created my purpose statement from the words I had selected: "To empower extraordinary unstoppable leadership."

I let my inspiration, enjoyments, and desires combine to determine my aim. I created my AIM Chart (page 84) and listed how, with whom, and where I could make a difference by fulfilling my purpose and, at the same time, developing and expanding myself.

AIM

HOW	WHO	WHERE
Teaching	Youth	Schools
Coaching	Adults	Communities
Writing	Teachers	Government
Speaking	Leaders	Business
Training	Counselors	Oregon
Event Planning		United States
		World

My deepest passion was seeing the leader within come alive—especially with young people—and I was ready to thrive. I was clear that I no longer wanted to be limited by my past. The need to hide my personal life from my professional life had disappeared and for the first time, I felt free to create the life I truly wanted. Richard Bach's quote, "You are never given a wish or dream without also being given the power to make it come true," became my daily reminder. Little did I know that my purpose was about to guide me in a new direction.

———————

Back in the Inventive Roost, Robert, Annabelle, and Hugh relax in the yard by the chicken coop. Let's listen in while Robert works with Hugh to invent his purpose.

"What did you learn about yourself from that lesson Hugh?" asks Robert.

"I see that I've been an emotional sheep without a personal purpose."

"There's nothing wrong with that," says Robert. "Just because you're a sheep, doesn't mean your mind, heart, and spirit can't have a purpose and aim. Stay true to your purpose, follow your spirit, live life fully . . ."

"Robert," shouts Hugh, "Can we get back to inventing my purpose?"

"Sorry, there I go again, jumping ahead. First, what do you want now in your life?"

"I want to make a difference when I return to my flock," says Hugh.

"Are you going back?" asks Annabelle.

"I am now that I know I have a choice."

"Excellent," says Robert. "What inspired you to make the choice to return home?" asks Robert.

"A feeling I have inside and the knowledge that I can choose to have personal power," says Hugh.

"That's fitting for a courageous sheep," he says. "How will you show your power?"

"By playing," says Hugh.

"What do you mean 'playing'?" asks Robert.

"I want to have fun with my power and play at the same time," says Hugh.

"That sounds interesting. What results do you want from power and play?"

"I want peace."

"How do you think power, play, and peace relate to each other?" asks Robert.

"Well," Hugh stops for a moment. "Courage gives me personal power. I don't want to rule others. I want to play with them and support them. That makes me feel peaceful and happy inside."

"A very nice purpose for a leader with harmonizing tendencies," says Annabelle.

"Who do you want to express your purpose with?" asks Robert.

"With children."

"You're a sheep. How can you do that? Besides, children don't have much power until they grow up," says Robert. "They are playful but not always peaceful."

"That's my point," says Hugh. "Back home, when I watched children play Follow the Leader, they seemed to sense their leader within. But some quit playing and I'm not sure why. If they grow up knowing about the Leadership Garden and these lessons, their personal power, playfulness, and inner peace will blossom. That would help grow a safer world, don't you think?" asks Hugh.

"A fabulous, marvelous, ingenious, stupendous, and superb idea," crows Robert.

"I can see it now." Hugh looks to the sky.

"Well, ya' know you've found your purpose when it makes you feel good and you can imagine great deeds. Is there anything you would like to add, Annabelle?" asks Robert.

"Only, that I love the moment when I see the grace and beauty of self-expression on a leader's face," says Annabelle.

"That's no surprise, with you as his tour guide," says Robert.

"Hugh, there are still a few more lessons to learn before you're ready to leave the farm and share your purpose and aim," says Annabelle. "Next, you'll meet Asli in the Quality Yard. Her name means genuine and real. She'll show you the qualities you need to fully express your leadership."

"That would be good, since I don't have a clue about how to do that," says Hugh.

Robert hops back on his perch. "Don't worry. You'll be great. Just be clear about your purpose and the rest will follow. Before you go, will you tell us the moral of this lesson?"

Hugh shouts, "Personal purpose and aim gives rise to my leader spirit."

Robert fans his tail feathers, spreads his wings, and hollers, "Look out world, here comes Hugh, a remarkable leader extraordinaire. . ."

Hugh picks up his Balance Wheel, Annabelle smiles at Robert, and the two run off toward the Quality Yard, Robert's voice growing faint in the distance.

INVENTIVE ROOST EXERCISE FIVE:

1. Create your E.A.R.S. chart in your guidebook. Start with *experience*. List what inspires you and what dispirits you.
2. Next, list *actions* you take daily, weekly, or monthly. List what you enjoy and what you avoid.
3. List the *results* you want and need in your life.
4. Pick the words that give you the most inspiration, joy, and desire from your three charts. Now play with those words and write your purpose statement, then continue with step five.
5. Finally, add *synergy* to determine your aim. List how, with whom, and where you want to express your purpose. Circle your targets (how, who, and where) and combine them with your purpose statement to create your aim.

Note: If you have trouble inventing a purpose that inspires you, you may have some hidden weeds or spirit blockers left in your Leadership Garden or leader behaviors you need to cultivate. Don't let what dispirits you or what you avoid, cloud your imagination. You may need to stew for a while and let this exercise simmer. If so, remember, purpose hatches new ways of being. Once you have your purpose, you will know and feel it.

6

QUALITY
YARD

Integrity brings out the quality

and greatness in leaders.

— Debra J. Slover

ANNABELLE RUNS TOWARD the Quality Yard, leaving Hugh in the dust. He drops his Balance Wheel and yells, "Annabelle, wait up."

She stops and looks back. "I'm sorry Hugh, your purpose and aim got me so excited that I lost sight of my job. I can't wait for you to meet Asli. She's a very special goose."

"Why's that?" asks Hugh, catching his breath.

"You'll find out," says Annabelle. "We're almost there; better pick up your Balance Wheel."

A beautiful white goose, covered with curly feathers, stands by a carved wooden gate that opens into the farmhouse yard. The scent of freshly mowed grass blends with the flowers around the edge of the yard.

"Hi, Annabelle, Hello Hugh," the goose says. "What a lovely Balance Wheel."

He puts his wheel down inside the gate. "How do you know my name? And why are your feathers so curly?" he asks, an embarrassed look on his face.

Asli beckons with her right wing. "Come my dear friends. Leda told me your name at lunch and that you and Annabelle were on your way," she says. "In answer to your other question, I'm a Sebastopol goose. My curly feathers don't allow me to fly like other geese. They ground me and help me see the essential qualities leaders need to work together. One quality is not being embarrassed to ask questions."

"I'm not embarrassed," he says.

Asli raises her hackles, tilts her head, and steps forward. Hugh leans back toward Annabelle. She shakes her head and nudges him forward.

"Okay—well maybe a little," Hugh says. "I'm not usually so direct."

Asli lowers her feathers. "Very good, Hugh. You admitted that you had told a fib when you said you weren't embarrassed. A leader who thrives always has the courage to tell the truth. Besides, the real you has nothing to hide."

"Asli, can you tell me if the purpose and aim that I invented is the real me?" he asks.

"Are you inspired by it?"

"When I think of my purpose, I get a tear in my eye, feel love in my heart, and I can see happy children on the playground growing strong."

Asli responds, "That's a sign your heart, mind, and spirit are united to unearth your purpose and aim. But the true test will be your integrity."

"What's that?"

"Let me show you." Asli takes Hugh and Annabelle over to her nesting hut. In the center, a glimmering egg rests on a small nest woven from twigs, straw, and Asli's white feathers. "Integrity is the golden egg of leadership," she says.

"How do I get one?"

"You already have it."

"I don't have any eggs," says Hugh. Annabelle and Asli start to laugh. "Why are you laughing?" he asks.

"We aren't laughing at you, just at your response," says Asli. "Let me explain. An old Aesop's Fable tells about a farmer who killed the goose that laid the golden egg. But when he killed it, he found the goose no different from other geese and there would be no more golden eggs."

"He doesn't sound like a very smart farmer," says Hugh.

"The farmer's greed for wealth and power is what also drives some leaders to do things they know are wrong or harmful," says Asli. "The golden egg of integrity in the Quality Yard is a symbol of your word, a leader's most prized possession."

Annabelle adds, "Integrity comes from honoring your word; it is the root of your power. When you act with integrity, you will thrive."

"Wow. That seems simple," says Hugh.

"On the surface it is, but for many leaders, behaving with integrity is difficult," says Asli.

"Why's that?" asks Hugh, shifting his hooves.

"When your garden is in a survival condition, you often make up excuses, cut corners, sell out, and may revert to blame and victimization. When you bring integrity to your purpose and aim, growing a thriving Leadership Garden becomes easy because you feel a sense of rightness," says Asli.

"What does rightness mean? Blossom talked about self-righteousness in the Nurturing Meadow but I thought she said it was a Leadership Garden disease," he says.

"Self-righteousness is one of the signs of victimization. That's not the same as rightness. When you have integrity, you feel good inside; if you loose your integrity, you feel bad. The feeling of rightness is a test of your integrity," says Asli.

"Now that you've invented your purpose and aim, if you slip back into a survival condition, you will feel it," says Annabelle. "Just like you did a few moments ago."

"What do I do if that happens again?"

"Be true to your word and tell the truth. If you're feeling bad, it's time to look for your golden egg," says Asli.

"I can see now why my word is so precious," he grins and looks over at Annabelle. She smiles back and nods to Asli. Annabelle thinks to herself, *he's got the message.*

"Along with integrity, there are seven common attributes that help bring quality to your life as a leader. Your success depends upon how you use them," Asli says.

"Attributes are already growing in my leadership garden?" he asks.

"Yes, they're in your Leader Balance Inventory. We'll look in the Quality Yard Lesson to find out more about integrity and the other attributes of leader behaviors," says Asli.

QUALITY YARD LESSON:

Those who stand for nothing fall for anything.
— Alexander Hamilton

Integrity, the next principle of the Leadership Garden, determines the quality of a leader. Leadership Gardens thrive with integrity, and wither and die without it. Regardless of your thoughts and feelings in the moment, you bring integrity to your garden when your words and actions are consistent with your purpose and aim.

I came face to face with my integrity when I began to write this book. I had been excited about taking on this new endeavor and had told my friends and family about my project. But over time I had became overwhelmed and wanted to quit. When asked about my book, I felt confronted and made excuses.

One day while out for a walk, something came to me: *I wanted to write a book about unstoppable leadership, but being afraid to tell the truth has stopped me in my tracks. What about my purpose and aim?* What a silly goose I was! I had forgotten my own lessons. My thoughts, feelings, emotions, and concerns were not going to go away, but now they had the power, not me.

I went back to work, restored my integrity, and my book is now in your hands. I found a wonderful quote by Anais Nin that spoke to that experience: "There came a time when the risk to remain tight in the bud was more painful than the risk it took to blossom."

Along with integrity, there are seven common attributes of leadership. Each attribute has several aspects and is an insight into the way we tend to express our leader behavior. But who we really are surfaces when we balance and blend the attributes to express our genuine purpose and aim with others. The attributes are defined as follows:

- **Communication:** Exchange of thoughts, ideas, information, and/or feelings
- **Cooperation:** Working with another for mutual benefit
- **Recognition:** State of being seen, known, or heard
- **Respect:** Acceptance, courtesy, or honor
- **Responsibility:** Accountability for thoughts, feelings, actions, or results
- **Teamwork:** Combined interest and talent of a group to achieve a common goal
- **Trust:** Reliance, integrity, certainty, or confidence

Keep in mind, the goals you set and the actions you take will not thrive without integrity, the guiding force that builds strength in you and trust with others. Integrity allows you to grow, expand, and develop the essential attributes needed to blossom leadership greatness.

Back in the Quality Yard, Asli is about to show Hugh how to pick new attributes when Annabelle hears Leda call her.

"Asli, I need to go to the barn to see what Leda wants. I'll be back soon," she says. Annabelle picks up Hugh's Balance Wheel by the gate and brings it to him. "You're going to need this," she says and dashes off. Asli waves goodbye to Annabelle and turns back to Hugh.

"Why does Leda want Annabelle?" asks Hugh.

"I'm not sure. Maybe her pups need her," says Asli. "They are almost grown now and Aristotle and Leda are preparing them to be guides, just like her," says Asli.

"With Annabelle as their mother, I'm sure they'll be great guides," he says.

"No doubt about it. But let's get back to your Leader Balance Inventory."

Hugh turns over his Balance Wheel to look at his Inventory.

"What choices among the attributes did you pick to create your Balance Wheel?" asks Asli.

He looks for a moment. "I'm afraid some of them might be weeds now that I have my purpose and aim."

"What you chose are weeds only if you are working from survival tendencies and they don't empower your purpose and aim," says Asli. "For example, my highest score on the Leader Balance Wheel used to be energize and my second harmonize." She looks off into the distance. "I was a know-it-all. Some of the other geese called me a silly goose. But when my mother taught me to say 'I feel,' rather than 'I know,' they began to trust me and listen to what I had to say."

"What is your purpose and aim, Asli?" he asks.

"To empower people to be playful, alive, and in love with life."

"I can see how being a know-it-all would spoil that."

"Exactly. I can only fulfill my purpose by really listening to what others have to say. Now I'm playful and silly without being a know-it-all, and I help others pick new choices among the attributes from the four leader behaviors that encourage their leader spirit," she says.

"You mean I don't have to stick with my original choices on my Leader Balance Inventory?"

"That's right," says Asli. "What's your purpose statement?"

"To teach children to be powerful, playful, peacemakers," he says.

"Very nice. What choices will you now pick to support that?" she asks.

Hugh looks at his Inventory, circles a few new choices, crosses some out, and finally picks:

- **Communication:** I feel and HOW?
- **Cooperation:** obey the rules and good listener
- **Recognition:** appreciative and loyal
- **Respect:** creative, structured, and change
- **Responsibility:** support and adventure
- **Teamwork:** practical and understanding
- **Trust:** depend upon

"Very good," says Asli. "You picked at least one attribute from each of the four leader behaviors. Now you can choose how you want to balance and blend them, kind of like picking a bouquet of beautiful flowers to blossom your purpose and aim."

"Can I pick and choose new ones anytime?"

"Yes, as long as you choose them with integrity. Otherwise, you'll pick and choose attribute behaviors on a whim or in reaction to a source event," she says. "There are at least four aspects of each attribute from which to choose, so if what you picked starts to wither, you'll want to pick something else. Just balance your behavior, stay true to your purpose, and hold onto your golden egg."

"I will, Asli," says Hugh.

"Now that you have your new bouquet of attributes, you can turn them into actions and results that will grow your garden stronger."

"How will I do that?"

"With commitment. Annabelle will take you to the Unstoppable Pasture where Howard the horse will teach you about that," says Asli.

As if on cue, Annabelle comes running in from the barn. "Are you ready Annabelle?" Asli calls out.

"You bet," she says, opening the gate. "Come on Hugh."

Hugh turns and smiles. "Bye Asli, thanks for helping me pick my bouquet. It's beautiful, just like you." Annabelle winks at Asli.

"That's kind of you to say," says Asli, "and you're very welcome." As Annabelle and Hugh start down the road, Asli calls from behind the gate, "Hugh, I forgot to have you tell us the moral of this lesson."

Hugh shouts back, "Integrity determines the quality of my leadership. Oh, and don't lose my golden egg."

Asli smiles and flaps her curly wings goodbye.

Hugh and Annabelle are on their way toward the Unstoppable Pasture when he stops and looks back. "Annabelle, I forgot my Balance Wheel with my new bouquet of attributes."

"No problem. We'll pick it up on the way back from our visit with Howard. Asli will keep an eye on it for now," says Annabelle. "I noticed you added your own thoughts again to the moral of the lesson. That's a sign that your Leadership Garden is truly beginning to bloom."

Hugh lifts his head and begins to strut down the path, as they continue on to the Unstoppable Pasture. Annabelle smiles and thinks, *he's finally found his pride and humor inside*.

QUALITY YARD EXERCISE SIX:

1. Write your purpose and aim on a blank sheet of paper in your guidebook.
2. To provide the first set of skills and practices for your purpose and aim, pick the attribute choices from the four leader behaviors on the following page and write them under your purpose. To use Asli's example in the fable, when she learned to say "I feel" instead of "I know," she chose to practice a new harmonize behavior to support her communication to fulfill her purpose.

Note: When you initially completed your Leader Balance Inventory on page 53, the choices you made in each row were from the attributes and relate to the leader behaviors.

Attributes	Visualize	Organize	Harmonize	Energize	Row
Communication	Asks "Why"	Asks "How"	Asks "Who"	Asks "What"	8
Communication	Says "I think"	Says "I should"	Says "I feel"	Says "I know"	11
Cooperation	Sets the rules	Enforces the rules	Obeys the rules	Avoids the rules	4
Cooperation	Problem solver	Sensible & logical	Good listener	Negotiater	1
Recognition	Competent	Loyal	Appreciative	Playful	3
Respect	Change	Results	Values	Freedom	9
Respect	Creative	Structured	Adaptable	Spontaneous	2
Responsibility	Pacesetter	Decision Maker	Supporter	Competitor	5
Responsibility	Initiative	Direction	Guidance	Adventure	12
Teamwork	Ideas	Process	Feelings	Action	6
Teamwork	Dreamer	Practical	Understanding	Casual	7
Trust	Build upon	Count on	Depend upon	Bet on	10

UNSTOPPABLE
PASTURE

Leaders who commit to a

genuine purpose and aim

will thrive in any

storm life has to offer.

— Debra J. Slover

Hugh and Annabelle pass by the barn on their way to meet Howard in the Unstoppable Pasture.

"Annabelle, what did Leda want?" asks Hugh.

"She wanted me to talk to my pups. Now that they're getting bigger, they're squabbling over who will lead and who will follow."

"Asli said they're going to be guides like you."

"That's right. They're ready to sprout their leader greatness but are having some growing pains and need to learn to honor differences. Now that they each have their purpose and aim, they think they know it all and have become critical of each other."

"Asli told me about her experience of being a know-it-all."

"Aristotle and Leda are taking my pups to Blossom to review leader-friendly gardening practices so I can work with you."

"I hope I'm not interfering with their lessons," he says.

"Absolutely not. My pups are going to be great guides. They just need practice and to learn how to keep their opinions and egos out of the way."

"What if the sheep back home are critical of my purpose and aim and don't understand my new behavior?"

"Naysayers have their own reality and you can't control what others think or how they feel and act," says Annabelle. "Remember, you're responsible for your own

behavior and how you choose to respond to your feelings.
Howard will show you how to be unstoppable and free
from doubt, fear, resignation, and cynicism."

"Why is he named Howard?"

"His name means heart, mind, brave, and hardy.
Howard knows the importance of being true to your spirit."

"What do you mean?" he asks.

Annabelle looks down at the ground. "Howard and his
herd were found in a pasture in the dead of winter. Their
owners had abandoned the farm, leaving the horses behind.
True to his name, Howard ran back and forth along the
fence line neighing for days."

"What happened? Hugh asks.

"Finally, the authorities came and all
the horses were brought back
to health and adopted.
That's how
Howard came
to the farm.
He's a hero to
have saved his herd.
I shudder to think of
what could've happened
without Howard's bravery."

"That's quite a story. I can't wait to meet him,
I've never met a hero before," says Hugh.

Hugh and Annabelle arrive to find Howard near the pond in the middle of the pasture; his shiny black coat glistens in the mid-afternoon sun.

"Howard, come meet Hugh." Howard runs through the grassy field toward Annabelle and Hugh.

"Good to see you again, Howard," says Annabelle. "This is Hugh, our newest leader."

"Nice to meet you, Leader Hugh. Have you enjoyed your tour so far?" asks Howard.

"Oh yes. Annabelle is a great guide and I have learned many valuable lessons."

"But you have doubts and fear," says Howard.

"How did you know that?"

"I'm a horse, I can sense doubt and fear in an instant," he says. "It takes courage, integrity, and commitment to be unstoppable when in pursuit of your purpose and aim. Doubts will pop up now and then, and fear is natural because you're discovering new behavior that's unfamiliar, but don't let that stop you."

"Howard, why do I have doubts and fear when my purpose and aim feels so right?" Hugh asks.

"You may have tried something new in the past and failed. You weren't born with doubts or fear. Have you ever noticed how fearless, free, and expressive young children are?"

"Yes, that is what I love about them," says Hugh. A smile crosses his face.

"Very young children also don't have boundaries," says Annabelle.

"That's right," says Howard. "We teach them boundaries to keep them safe. But sometimes boundaries grow into barriers and those barriers can turn into doubt." Howard flicks a fly away with his mane. "Doubts often surface from past failures and what others tell us. Feeding on fear or doubt, your own or others, will choke out your purpose and aim."

"I hope mine doesn't get choked when I go back home," says Hugh.

"There's no need to be concerned. Let's head out to the pond, you two look like you could use a drink of water. The Unstoppable Pasture Lesson should ease your mind and this'll be a good time to reflect on what you've learned so far."

UNSTOPPABLE PASTURE LESSON:

The only limit to our realization of tomorrow
will be our doubts of today.
— **Franklin D. Roosevelt**

Commitment is the next principle in the Leadership Garden. We begin this lesson by looking at physical, social, emotional, and spiritual boundaries that are designed to provide protection, safety, and order to life, and are necessary for basic survival. Some of these boundaries are:

- Physical needs such as food, clothing, shelter, and health
- Social laws and norms that govern society
- Emotional connections and interactions with others
- Spiritual beliefs and values that guide our conscience

To thrive, it is important to understand and respect these boundaries. Our focus in this chapter will be on self-imposed emotional boundaries that turn into barriers of self-doubt, fear of failure, resignation, or cynicism. These barriers suppress the leader spirit and stunt our growth.

It's useful to look at opposing views, but when we're in a thriving condition we don't let the views of others sway us from our unique purpose and aim. Because unexpected setbacks and obstacles often occur, and failure is a part of life, we may find ourselves in a survival condition, resigned and cynical. Setbacks, failure, and disappointments are to be expected and thriving leaders use them as an opportunity to grow and expand.

I mentioned earlier that my embarrassment about being confronted almost stopped me from completing this book. I had tried to protect myself from criticism. After I had spent months researching, rewriting, and working with my editor, I asked my friend, Edwardo, to give me his honest opinion of a few chapters. A few days later, he called me. "This sounds like a research paper versus your story in a fable. Trust yourself and speak from your heart," he said.

After all my hard work, I wanted to resist his analysis. But he was right; he had sensed my doubt. I had been using others to validate my point of view, rather than speaking for myself. Letting go of my doubt freed my voice and leader spirit.

Unstoppable commitment, with integrity to our unique purpose and aim, counterbalances our barriers, and inspires and frees our leader spirit. But being unstoppable does not give us license to be stubborn or foolish. It is one thing to *say* we are committed to something and yet another to *be* committed enough to stand up for it. The key to being unstoppable is to let go of our ego and follow four essential steps I call the "Circle of Commitment": declare, act, complete, and celebrate.

Using all four leader behaviors helps us move through the Circle with ease. However, when we are under stress or up against deadlines, it's easy to revert back to familiar behavior, and we may get stuck. Below are the leader behaviors and the phases for each that could cause problems:

- **Visualize**—declaration phase. New ideas and projects are easy, but committing the time and resources to complete them and then celebrate is a challenge.
- **Energize**—action phase. There is a tendency to abandon the project if it isn't fun or doesn't have enough action.

- **Organize**—completion phase. The desire to produce results overrides the need to celebrate and experience the joy of the process.
- **Harmonize**—celebration phase. There is a tendency to revel in the joy and to resist getting back to business.

In addition to these problems, there is another hidden barrier to commitment, what I call the, "Commitment Paradox." Most leadership comes with a sense of obligation and attachment, but a thriving leader commits to a purpose and aim without either. The commitment paradox relates to our integrity. In a survival condition, our integrity is compromised by obligation that turns into martyrdom and/or an attachment to an outcome that limits our ability to be flexible and adaptable, and that's when we may find ourselves stopped.

Commitment Paradox

When I moved the OSSOM program into my home, I remained uncertain and resigned about my decision. In the process of writing this book, I began to realize that my identity was still attached to the program and I felt obligated to the youth. I was caught in the declaring phase and was being a martyr. But when I recognized these issues and chose to let them go and move on, a new opportunity emerged when a former student contacted me and wanted to do an internship with OSSOM. We worked together and nine months later, OSSOM was ready for rebirth under her leadership.

When we give up unwholesome attachments and obligations, live our lives with integrity, and are true to our purpose and aim, unforeseen opportunities will emerge and results will occur. Since every leader faces obstacles, setbacks, and disagreement from others, the question is, will we give up, survive, or thrive? Even when faced with what seems like insurmountable odds, our leader thrives when we remove our self-imposed barriers and remain steadfast, flexible, and open to our unique purpose and aim.

Back in the pasture, the afternoon sun sparkles on the pond. Hugh talks to Howard and Annabelle about what he's learned in this lesson.

"Now do you see the emotional barriers and doubts that have stopped you in the past?" asks Howard.

"Yes. When I came here, I was a scared sheep, wandering alone through life. I thought being alone and timid was my destiny. When I was drinking from the pond, I looked at my refection and saw that I had become a bold, courageous, loving sheep, ready to be with people and take action," Hugh says.

"How does it feel?" asks Annabelle.

"Great. Since I removed the weeds and spirit blockers in my garden, I feel free to express my true leader," says Hugh.

Howard nods his head, "Verrrry nice. Seeing yourself and the world through new eyes is exciting. But you're not done yet, there's more to see. Before you leave here, do you have any questions?"

"Just one. I understand about doubt, but what about resignation and cynicism?"

"Remember, I said that you weren't born with doubt," says Howard. "You weren't born resigned or cynical, either. Those behaviors grow over time, usually after setbacks and disappointments that harden the heart, restrain the mind, and suppress the spirit."

"It seems sad to live life resigned and cynical," says Hugh.

"It is," says Howard. "You can lead the way to thriving."

Annabelle adds, "To create a thriving future, you want to make sure that what you're doing and how you're behaving line up with your purpose and aim. That's your integrity."

"That's sound advice, Annabelle," says Howard. "Always let integrity be your guide to unstoppable commitment."

Annabelle walks toward the fence and Howard continues to talk with Hugh.

"Now that you are ready to move on, Allegra will show you how to express your purpose and aim with others. She is a lively pig and full of expression," says 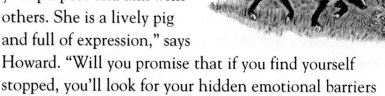 Howard. "Will you promise that if you find yourself stopped, you'll look for your hidden emotional barriers and remove them?"

"I promise," says Hugh. "I am committed to teaching children to be powerful, playful, peacemakers. I can hardly wait to get started."

"Now that's a thriving leader." Howard looks at Annabelle, near the fence. "Hugh is ready to go meet Allegra," he nickers. Annabelle runs back, wagging her tail.

"What were you doing, Annabelle?" asks Hugh.

"Sniffing for more doubt, but luckily, I didn't find any," she says. "You are going to love Allegra. But I must warn you, she doesn't mess around with her commitment to full leadership expression. Let's go, times a wasting."

"Before you leave, can you tell us the moral of this lesson?" asks Howard.

"Of course," says Hugh. "I commit to make a positive difference in the world using my unique purpose and aim."

"Excellent, Leader Hugh," says Howard. "Be off now to make your difference."

Hugh and Annabelle rush off to the Expression Pen, their last stop on the tour.

UNSTOPPABLE PASTURE EXERCISE SEVEN:

1. In your guidebook, list the emotional barriers that may stop you from committing to your purpose and aim. Look at where you're attached to an outcome or feel obligated.
2. Identify where you may be caught in the Circle of Commitment, based upon your leader behavior tendencies.
3. Now take the action step of commitment to your purpose and aim. Set some goals and create a list of actions with a deadline.

8

EXPRESSION
PEN

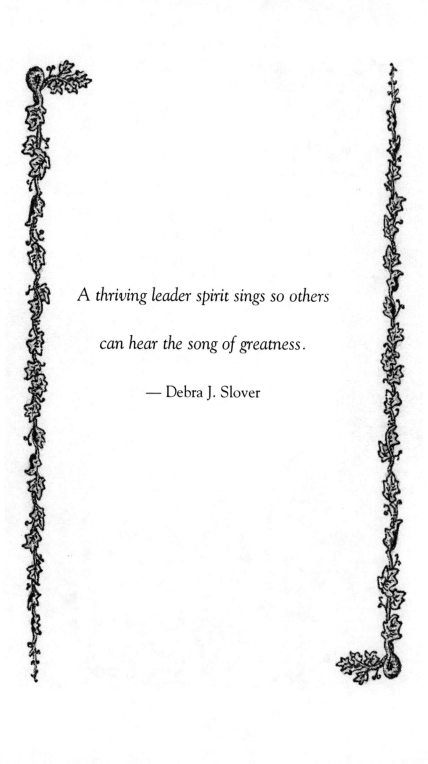

A thriving leader spirit sings so others

can hear the song of greatness.

— Debra J. Slover

Hugh sprints ahead, Annabelle trailing behind.

"Hurry up," calls Hugh. "I want to get there. I have a long journey home and I want to start soon as possible."

"Slow down, Hugh," yells Annabelle, "I can barely keep up with you and we need to stop and pick up your Balance Wheel."

When they reach the Integrity Yard, Hugh's Balance Wheel is hanging on the gate. Annabelle whispers, "Asli must be nesting. Quietly remove your wheel and we'll move on."

"But Annabelle, my wheel looks different," he murmurs.

"When you picked new attributes for your purpose and aim, your four leader behaviors were rebalanced. Asli must've fixed it for you."

"That was nice of her," he says.

The breeze has died down; the shadows grow long in the late afternoon. When Hugh and Annabelle arrive at the Expression Pen, Allegra, a bright pink sow, is at the feeding trough. She walks over to the water barrel where Annabelle and Hugh have stopped to rest.

"Annabelle, I'm so glad to see you, but you look exhausted," Allegra says.

Annabelle stretches her neck. "Allegra, we've had a busy day. Hugh has become quite a go-getter, and with his energy, he'll make a great leader." Annabelle takes a drink from the barrel and walks off to find some shade. Hugh begins to follow her.

Allegra calls out. "Hugh, where are you going?"

He drops his Balance Wheel and says, "I want to make sure Annabelle's okay."

"She's fine. Come now, we have work to do," says Allegra.

Allegra and Hugh walk over to the shed by the trough. "Okay Hugh, I want to check the condition of your Leadership Garden," she says.

"Have you planted your new seeds and pulled your weeds?"

"Yes, ma'am."

"Are your spirit blockers gone?"

Hugh glances over at Annabelle, resting in the shade.

"Don't look to her, you can speak for yourself," says Allegra.

"Okay, I mean, yes ma'am." he replies.

"Do you know your leader behavior tendencies?"

"Yes, ma'am and my wheel is rebalanced."

"Good. Now, are your E.A.R.S. clear?"

"Yes, ma'am!" says Hugh, lifting his ears.

"Now you're showing some spunk," says Allegra. "Do you have your golden egg?"

"You bet," he says with a chuckle.

"Are you truly committed to fulfill your purpose and aim?"

"Absolutely!"

"Very good," says Allegra. "So you're out to make a difference with children, to teach them to be powerful, playful, peacemakers, to grow a safer world," Allegra says.

"That's correct," says Hugh.

"How do you propose to do that?"

"On the playground near my home," he says.

"That wasn't my question," snorts Allegra. "I asked you how. You told me where."

"Oops," he says. "Sorry."

"Don't apologize. Not paying attention is common among survival leaders. To be a great leader and thrive, you need to listen and speak your voice with confidence and pride."

"But Annabelle said I'm going to be a great leader."

"That's what she said, but what do you say?" Allegra asks.

"I'm an unstoppable leader with a unique purpose and aim," shouts Hugh.

"Excellent. Here in the Expression Pen you'll learn something very important, the art of communication and how to express yourself effectively. It may be your last lesson, but it's a very important one. So listen up," commands Allegra.

EXPRESSION PEN LESSON:

Self-expression must pass into communication
for its fulfillment.
— Pearl S. Buck

This book began with my Leadership Garden Legacy quote about sprouting greatness. Greatness sprouts from our self-expression through communication, the last principle of the Leadership Garden. Our unique self-expression blossoms when our purpose and aim bind our heart, mind, and spirit into a new way of being that communicates greatness.

Defined in Chapter Six, communication is the exchange of thoughts, ideas, information, or feelings that occur through our words, listening ability, and behavior. Communication is the instrument of our integrity and the other attributes of leadership.

In a survival condition, our integrity is compromised by how we listen, speak, and react to our thoughts. Those reactions and thoughts are controlled by our past experiences, a vantage point from which we can only compare, assess, and judge what we hear and see. What's actually said and happening around us is lost and we miss the opportunity to see, hear, learn, and imagine anything new.

The weeds growing in our garden that we have discussed in the previous chapters, block our ability to listen. We remove these weeds when we learn to communicate new thoughts, feelings, and actions that demonstrate our greatness and open the door for the greatness of others. Transforming *how* we listen and *what* we listen for, creates a new opportunity for our words and actions.

When we hear, see, think about, and respond to excitement or stress with our words and actions, our dominant verbal communication tendencies may take over. Below is a list of those tendencies for each leader behavior:

- **Visualize** says, "I think," and asks, "Why?"
- **Organize** says, "I should," and asks, "How?"
- **Harmonize** says, "I feel," and asks, "Who?"
- **Energize** says, "I know," and asks, "What?"

Practicing our purpose and aim with integrity creates a condition for greatness; we facilitate (or support) better communication and behaviors that nurture the greatness of ourselves and others.

On my last day at the university, I pulled up to the campus kiosk where a student I hadn't seen before was working. "I'm cleaning out my office today and I need a daylong loading pass," I said to her.

"I'm sorry, but I'm only authorized to give 20 minute passes. You'll have to go to parking services," she said. I became annoyed, glared at her, and drove away to get my pass. When I returned to my vehicle with my loading pass, I began to cry. I realized I'd been a jerk to project my attitude onto the student. I didn't want to start my last day like this; my behavior was not consistent with who I wanted to be.

I drove back to the kiosk. "I would like to apologize for my behavior. I pride myself on being great with others. You were just doing your job and I wasn't great with you. I hope you have a wonderful day," I told her. A lovely smile crossed the student's face.

"You have a wonderful day too," she said. My spirit was lifted when I took responsibility for my behavior, remaining true to my purpose and aim.

When we paint a picture in our mind of what's possible to achieve with our purpose and aim—the essence of who we are—we listen for, speak to, and respond to only that image. If our communication touches the mind, heart, and spirit of others, they naturally join in. If not, we take responsibility for our failed communication to restore our power. Who we are and what we listen for, combined with how we listen, think, speak, and behave, creates the synergy for greatness. One idea leads to another, which leads to action, and actions that grow in harmony with others, sprout our greatness.

Growing and nurturing a thriving Leadership Garden enables us to clear our mind and re-write our story, giving us the ability to hear and speak our unique voice. When we choose to become a leader with purpose and aim, and practice the principles and exercises in this book, we will thrive and our garden, and the gardens of others, will flourish.

——————

Back in the Expression Pen, Allegra makes sure Hugh is ready for his journey home. Annabelle takes a well-deserved nap in the shade.

"Now do you see why I questioned you when you arrived?" asks Allegra.

"I think so," says Hugh.

"I wanted to make sure that you had completed your lessons."

"Well, I thought you were kind of stern because you asked me so many questions," he says. "But now I see you just wanted to make sure I understood my lessons so I can be great."

"That's right. My job before you leave here is to root out any weeds left in your garden and to show you how to communicate. 'Be direct and don't mess around with your purpose and aim,' that's my motto," says Allegra. "You access your greatness by how you listen. That's what Robert meant when he talked about hatching new ways of being. Your purpose and aim gives you a new place to look, listen, and experience the world."

"I think I get it. If I listen for my purpose and aim, that's what I will experience and see, and how I'll be with others."

"Exactly. Others will hear it, see it, and join you."

"Wow. I hadn't thought of it that way. Now I know how to lead the way to power, peace, and play."

Annabelle opens an eye and glances at Hugh. *He's passed Allegra's test and is an unstoppable and inspiring leader now.*

"That's right," says Allegra. "Use the Leadership Garden principles and practices to sing your unique song. Your aim may shift and grow through time as you share with others, but stay true to your purpose."

"My purpose is leading me back home where I have some unfinished business. I need to let my flock know I'm okay, and I want to find out what happened to my mom. That'll give me peace."

"Completing your unfinished business will open the door to your new journey," says Allegra. "You've now found your unique place to roost, just like Robert said you would," she says softly.

"I sure have," he replies. "I can feel it."

"Are there any last questions I can answer for you about the U.N.I.Q.U.E. lessons and Leadership Garden before you leave here?" asks Allegra.

"Nope," says Hugh. "I'm a bold, courageous, and loving sheep with a clear purpose and aim that I will communicate with everyone I meet. It is my commitment and what I'll honor as my truest self."

"Extraordinary," squeals Allegra. "Can you tell us the moral of this lesson before we go to the barn and meet up with the others for your special surprise?"

"But I think Annabelle's asleep. I don't want her to miss my surprise."

Annabelle stretches her legs and stands up. "I'm awake, Hugh. I heard everything. I was just taking a moment for myself," she says. "Now tell us the moral of this lesson."

Hugh lifts his head and puffs his chest out, "Express my unique leader spirit in the world."

"Excellent." says Allegra. "Let's head to the barn."

A cool westerly breeze has picked up and the sun is setting behind the barn. When the three arrive, Leda, Aristotle, George, Blossom, Robert, Asli, and Howard are waiting by a platform of hay bales on the side of the barn. Leda and Aristotle join hands and step onto the platform. Aristotle motions for Hugh and Annabelle to join them. Annabelle takes Hugh's Balance Wheel and holds it up for all to see, then hands it to Leda, who posts it behind her on the hay bale.

"It's customary on the Leadership Farm to send you on your journey with a U.N.I.Q.U.E. collar and a bell that will ring throughout the world," says Aristotle.

Leda bends down and places a beautiful black collar, embroidered with a green and gold leader vine, around Hugh's neck.

"This collar and bell symbolize a quote from dancer and choreographer Martha Graham. 'There is vitality, a life force, an energy, a quickening, that is translated through you into action, and because there is only one you in all time, this expression is unique. And if you block it, it will never exist through any other medium and will be lost.' Hugh, let your bell ring and never forget you are a unique leader in the world," says Leda.

Aristotle looks out at the other animals. "When Hugh wandered onto the Leadership Farm he was lost. But he learned his U.N.I.Q.U.E. leadership expression from all of you. He's now a noble sheep, bold and courageous with a unique purpose and aim, never to be lost again."

Leda and Aristotle clap. The animals shout and cheer. "Yeah, Hugh! Three cheers for our new leader!" Hugh looks out at all his new friends and smiles.

After a few moments, Leda lifts her hand to quiet them. "Hugh, can you tell us the moral of this book?"

"Yes," says Hugh. "Express my unique leader voice, loud and clear, so others will sprout greatness far and near."

Everyone cheers again.

"Well spoken, Hugh." Robert crows, "Listen up world, here comes Hugh, he's ready to sing his unique song . . ."

"Shush Robert, you're stealing Hugh's moment," scolds Howard.

Everyone nods and looks back at Hugh.

"Hugh, the other animals told us you have learned your lessons well and your leader behaviors are now perfectly balanced for your purpose and aim," says Leda.

Annabelle walks over to Hugh and rests her paw on his shoulder. "I am the favor, grace, and beauty of life and you are the heart, mind, and spirit. To support you on your journey, I will join you as your partner," she says.

Allegra snorts, Howard kicks his hind legs, Asli flaps her wings, and Blossom flicks her tail. George butts the hay bale and knocks Robert from his perch. Robert jumps up and shakes his head.

Annabelle had already told Aristotle and Leda that the time had come for her to leave the farm and take a new journey, but she chose to tell the others with Hugh. "My dear friends," she says, "after working with Hugh and each of you today, I caught a glimpse of a new dawn. Thanks to you, Hugh has emerged into a unique leader that has re-ignited my spirit. Together, we will protect each other and teach the children of the world how to sprout greatness."

"Are you sure you want to leave, Annabelle?" asks George.

"I'm not leaving. My spirit lives on in my pups and in each of you," she says. "That is the nature and miracle of life I have come to understand."

"I'd love to have you join me on my new journey, Annabelle," replies Hugh. He looks out at the other animals. "How I can ever repay you for what you've given me."

"There's no need. Empower each other, sing your voices, and together, do good work on behalf of all children of the world," shouts Allegra.

Annabelle and Leda smile at each other and the four step down from the platform. The animals gather around Hugh to give him a few last words of advice.

Annabelle slips away into the barn. She lies down by her pups and nuzzles each one. "My dear children, I'm going on an important new journey with Hugh."

"What will happen to us?" whimpers one of her pups.

"One of you will become the new tour guide on the farm and the rest of you will leave soon to be guides on other Leadership Farms," she says.

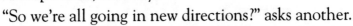

"So we're all going in new directions?" asks another.

"Yes, and as you travel your new path, keep love in your heart and hope in your spirit."

"We understand Mother," one says.

"Can we meet Hugh before you leave?" another asks.

"Certainly, come with me."

Annabelle rejoins Hugh outside the barn. She introduces her pups, one by one. "This is Uri, Naomi, Ingeborg, Quique, Urho, and Euphemia. The first letter of their names spells UNIQUE, just like the lessons and, as you've learned Hugh, being unique is the favor, grace, and beauty of life."

Hugh looks down at the pups, tumbling and playing near their mother. "You're lucky pups to have a mother like Annabelle. I know you'll be great leader guides, just like your mom."

Annabelle smiles at Hugh and turns to her pups. "Settle down now. The sun is setting and it's time for me and Hugh to start our journey. I love you all and know you are strong and brave." She licks each on the forehead. "Nurture your Leadership Gardens and be true to your unique purpose and aim."

"Annabelle, are you okay?" asks Hugh.

"Yes," she says quietly. "It's never easy to leave those you love, but I taught my pups to appreciate nature, weather the change of seasons, and thrive."

Hugh and Annabelle wave good-bye to everyone and head into the sunset, down the lane that brought Hugh to the Leadership Farm.

Stay tuned. Hugh and Annabelle's U.N.I.Q.U.E. tour with the children of the world has just begun.

Not all those who wander are lost.

— J.R.R. Tolkien

EXPRESSION PEN EXERCISE 8:

Congratulations. You have now completed the first step of *U.N.I.Q.U.E. Growing Your Leader Within*. The direction you head and what you see and listen for will guide your behavior. The power you have in your heart, mind, and spirit to choose your legacy and write your life story is the favor, grace, and beauty of life. To support you on your new journey complete this final exercise.

1. Go back to the first two pages in your guidebook. Now that you have your purpose and aim, it is time to take action. Make a list of opportunities that you now see. What will you do and with whom will you communicate your purpose and aim? Begin with what you truly want in your life.
2. Next, make a list of any unfinished business you would like to complete and with whom you would like to communicate.
3. Once you have identified those opportunities, make a list of people you will share your purpose and aim with, and then ask for their support.
4. Then honor your word to yourself and communicate with those you need to complete unfinished business and those you want to support you.

Endnote: By taking 100% responsibility to guide and direct your life and using the principles and practices of this book, I promise you will be amazed at the unforeseen opportunities that will come your way and the results that will sprout from your greatness. I would love to hear what you discover. To learn how to share your story, go to: The Future—EMPOWER THE SEEDS OF LEADERSHIP GREATNESS on page 143.

EPILOGUE

Throughout my life, I have had the opportunity to work with, know, and love many great leaders. Most are not the ones you read about—they are people like you and me, who give the extraordinary gift of their unique self-expression.

I began to write this book with one thought in mind: to unearth the unique leadership spirit of each person to be empowered, extraordinary, and unstoppable in life.

My inquiry started with my mother's leadership spirit that I felt went undiscovered. Yet I was humbled to learn that I was the one who had not fully discovered my own spirit. I thought about what I had learned from her and from each person I had met. Everywhere I looked, I saw some unique gift they had given me. And in the end, I came home to who I am; someone committed to sprout leadership greatness in the world's garden.

When I arrived home, inner peace, power, and vitality to play like a child again surfaced. I found a new appreciation for life's journey as a never-ending story. My original intention was to have Hugh's mother survive, as a surprise. But as I wrote the closing paragraphs, my mother's spirit spoke through Annabelle. My spirit lives on in you. I then knew how this story would end.

My friend Edwardo, mentioned in Chapter Seven, died at the young age of 41, before I finished this book. We often said that leadership is not about us, but about making a difference with others. Yet leadership is all about how we lead our life, for how can we make a difference with others, if we don't know how important we are and the profound impact we have on those around us? The true essence of life is to know who we are, experience the difference we make, and to thrive on the journey. I communicated Edwardo's leadership legacy through Asli; the wisdom of his words ring true in the world.

As you embark on your new journey of unique leadership expression with purpose and aim, I leave you with Edwardo's last words to me, "Keep the drafts coming. I truly enjoy witnessing the creative process. It's like witnessing God, for me. I love you."

U.N.I.Q.U.E.
LEADERSHIP GARDEN

The miracle of life is to thrive on the

journey with purpose and aim;

the endnote is our spirit lives on.

— Debra. J. Slover

Acknowledgements

I'd like to thank the following for their contributions to this book and to my life journey:

- My husband Terry, for his patience, insight, support, and unending faith in my ability.
- My children, stepchildren, their spouses, and grandchildren for creating together our thriving family Leadership Garden.
- Steve, my ex-husband and Terry's ex-wife Karen, for our children; the gift we share.
- Jodi Henry, of Writers Welcome, my editor, writing coach, teacher, and confidant.
- Donna Barnard, my publicist, whose guidance, direction, and contribution have been priceless.
- Darlene Warner, my illustrator, for her extraordinary artistic and creative talents.
- Michele DeFilippo, of 1106 Design, for her exquisite cover and interior book design.

- My friends, family, and colleagues who read my early
  manuscript drafts and provided encouragement and
  valuable critiques: Garnet Ascher, Cathy Baird,
  Lynn Chiotti, Everett Cutter, Darlene Dawson,
  Marty Dawson, Pauline Edinger, Gwyneth Green,
  Alison Hammett-Cummings, Georgiana Kovell-
  Freeman, Richard Hay, Kathy Nellist, Toni Newby,
  Debbie Sharpe, Katie Slover, Wes Walters, and
  Sue Weekly.

THE FUTURE—EMPOWER THE SEEDS OF LEADERSHIP GREATNESS

It is my hope that the Leadership Garden Legacy sprouts greatness in the heart, mind, and spirit of youth and adults everywhere. To support this effort, be on the lookout for the upcoming children's version of *U.N.I.Q.U.E: Growing the Leader Within.*

I also want to hear about your leadership experiences; your stories, desires, and accomplishments. To share your experiences, or to order this book in bulk, you can mail, fax, or e-mail:

Leader Garden Press
P.O. Box 841
Albany, OR 97321
Fax: 541-926-3524
E-mail: info@leadergardenpress.com
Website: www.leadergardenpress.com

For information about leadership training services, visit:
www.synergyinmotion.info

You Can Help Empower the Future

In Chapter Seven, you learned that when a leader gives up unwholesome attachments and obligations, unforeseen opportunities emerge. Writing and publishing *U.N.I.Q.U.E: Growing the Leader Within* has given me the opportunity to donate a portion of the proceeds to support the work of OSSOM and Hands to Heart International, a nonprofit started by one of my former OSSOM staff members. Through their unique and extraordinary leadership, these charitable organizations help sprout the seeds of greatness in children.

Operation Student Safety On the Move (OSSOM):

OSSOM, Inc., a nonprofit organization designed to empower youth leadership, promotes safe and healthy communities during the transition from adolescence to young adulthood. It operates from the premise of what if every child:

— knew that they could make a positive difference
— took responsibility for their actions, attitude, and choices
—was given the skills and opportunities to impact the lives of their peers

It is truly OSSOM (pronounced like AWESOME). To learn more, visit: www.ossom.org

HANDS TO HEARTS INTERNATIONAL (HHI):

HHI is a nonprofit organization dedicated to improving the health and well-being of orphaned children and economically disadvantaged women around the globe. HHI transforms orphanage care by training and then employing local women in the language, social, cognitive, and physical skills necessary for healthy early childhood development. Trainees learn how they can promote a child's growth in each area as well as the vital importance of attachment and bonding. Women hired by HHI provide individualized nanny-like care to two to four babies/children awaiting their adoptive families. To learn more, visit: www.handstohearts.org

ABOUT THE AUTHOR

Debra Slover graduated from Oregon State University with a degree in Health Education. She began her career as a high school teacher and later served as Director of Oregon Student Safety On the Move (OSSOM) for more than 20 years.

Debra is passionate about the possibilities available to youth and adults when given the skills, recognition, and opportunity to express their leadership voices. She founded Synergy in Motion in 2003 to bring vision, relationship, creativity, and a sense of playfulness to leadership by empowering the human spirit. Debra created Leader Garden Press in 2006 to advance this work.

Debra wrote this book using the 27 years of experience she gained training, empowering, and serving over 40,000 youth and adult leaders. During this time, she coordinated youth-led statewide conferences, leadership camps, and national conferences. She has been a presenter at numerous national, statewide, and local conferences and seminars, and has served as President of the National Association of Teen Institutes and Chair of the Oregon Coalition to Reduce Underage Drinking.

Debra lives in Albany, Oregon with her husband Terry and dog Mooko.

Printed in the United States
64309LVS00001B/79-174